BOOK OF EVERYTHING

BURSTING WITH THOUSANDS OF FANTASTIC FACTS

AUTUMN PUBLISHING

CONTENTS:

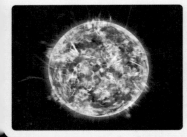   

WILDLIFE.................................92

ABOUT MYSELF.................................126

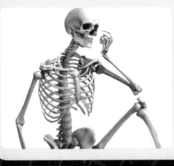 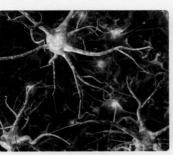  

SCIENCE.................................150

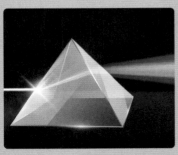   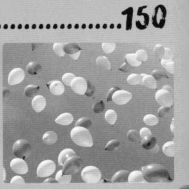

OUR ENDANGERED WORLD.................................172

  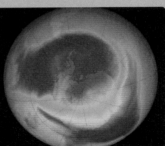 

THE UNIVERSE

NOTHING IS BIGGER

THE UNIVERSE COMPRISES EVERYTHING

The Earth, every person and thing on it, our solar system, the Milky Way, all the other galaxies, whether we can see them or not, even empty space . . . all these make up the Universe. It is the biggest thing that can be expressed in a single word.

HAVE YOU EVER WONDERED . . .

HOW MANY STARS ARE THERE?

More than you could possibly count. Scientists estimate that there are about 1.8 trillion stars for every human being alive in the world today!

The Universe is too vast to even imagine. It contains trillions of galaxies, stars, planets, nebulae, black holes, and just unlimited empty space.

Earth is NOT at the heart of the Universe

At one time people thought that Earth was at the center of the Universe, but now we know that Earth is only one of billions of planets moving through space.

NOTHING TRAVELS AS FAST AS LIGHT

Even if we could travel at the speed of light, which is the fastest known speed at which anything travels, it would take at least 15 billion years to cross the Universe—as far as we know! It's hard to say for sure because we can't even see the Universe's edges.

AMAZING!

The Universe is so big that it cannot be measured in miles. Even if we did, somehow, manage to travel beyond it, scientists are pretty sure that there could be no time, distance, absolutely nothing outside its boundaries.

The shape of the Universe is . . .

For many years it was believed that the Universe was round, like a blown-up balloon. But some scientists now think it might be flat—sort of like a pancake!

THE BIG BANG

THE BIG BANG RELEASED HUGE AMOUNTS OF ENERGY

All the mass and energy in our Universe was created in less than a second—in one huge, super-hot explosion. It was so hot that scientists don't even bother writing out all the zeros in the temperature. They write it as 10^{32} degrees Centigrade, meaning 10 multiplied 32 times!

Giant clouds of gases and particles, called nebulae, formed as the Universe cooled down after the Big Bang.

300 million years

Big Bang 0

380,000 years

A Big Crunch lies in the future

Some scientists think that billions of years in the future, the Universe will collapse inwards and end in a Big Crunch! But it may not be the end, because other scientists believe that even if there is a Big Crunch it will be followed by another Big Bang and a brand-new Universe will be born.

AMAZING!

You can still see the light generated by the Big Bang. If you look through a really powerful telescope, you will be able to see light from the other side of the Universe that began its journey just after the Big Bang.

It happened a very, very long time ago

Exactly when this Big Bang occurred has been argued about for centuries. Most scientists today agree that the Universe was born between 12 and 15 billion years ago.

There could be other universes being born.

MILLIONS OF UNIVERSES MAY BE IN THE MAKING

While it could not happen again in our Universe, it is possible that big bangs could be taking place millions of times, creating millions of different universes. It's unlikely that many would last as long as ours though—most would pop like soap bubbles.

Time →

HOW POWERFUL THE BIG BANG ACTUALLY WAS?

It was so powerful that the Universe is still expanding!

Over time, the Universe has changed. In the darkness that followed the Big Bang, stars appeared, then galaxies. And still more galaxies are being formed today!

GALAXIES GALORE

THERE ARE MORE THAN TWO TRILLION GALAXIES . . .

. . . and new ones are forming right now at the edges of the Universe!

A galaxy is a group of stars, dust, and gases that are held together by gravity. There are probably more than one quadrillion stars in the trillions of galaxies that make up the Universe.

AMAZING!

Our galaxy looks like a giant Danish pastry. Called the Milky Way, our galaxy is a huge spiral with swirls of what look like white icing. From above, it resembles a pastry. From the side, however, it looks more like two fried eggs stuck back to back.

We live at the edge of the Milky Way

Our solar system is located on one of the spiraling arms of the galaxy. According to scientists, there is probably a monster black hole at the center of the Milky Way, which is a million times bigger than our Sun!

Each galaxy is unlike any other

Some are bright and some are dim, and they are categorized into three basic galaxy shapes: spiral, elliptical (oval), and irregular. Of course, because "irregular" just means a galaxy has no particular shape, it is really a catch-all category!

The Universe is teeming with galaxies.

OUR GALAXY HAS A TWIN

Named Andromeda, it is the biggest galaxy near ours. Andromeda is about the same age as the Milky Way and has a similar shape, but contains many more stars.

HAVE YOU EVER WONDERED...

WHY OUR GALAXY IS CALLED THE MILKY WAY?

Look up on a clear night and you may be able to see for yourself. The 100 billion stars in the galaxy make it look like a milky band of starlight stretching across the sky.

THE SOLAR SYSTEM

In the 17th century, the scientist Galileo created a telescope and used it to make many discoveries about the solar system.

Sun

Mercury

Venus

OUR SOLAR SYSTEM IS THE SUM OF MANY PARTS

The word "solar" means "of the Sun," and the center of the solar system is the Sun. Around it orbit eight planets, which travel a set path. Also part of the solar system are the moons of these planets, and smaller objects such as comets, asteroids, and pieces of space rock that float around.

HAVE YOU EVER WONDERED ...

HOW BIG IS THE SOLAR SYSTEM?

If you consider the farthest reaches of the Sun's gravitational pull, the solar system could be as big as 11.8 trillion miles!

Neptune

Uranus

The Sun keeps everything together

The Sun has a powerful attraction: it pulls the different objects in the solar system toward it with an invisible force called gravity. This force keeps the planets spinning in orbit and prevents them from flying off into deepest space. Each planet also has its own gravitational force that keeps its moons close by.

Earth

Mars

Jupiter

Saturn

Planets orbit the Sun.

GOING AROUND THE SUN TAKES MANY DAYS

The closer a planet is to the Sun, the shorter and speedier its round trip. As the Sun's nearest neighbor, Mercury whizzes around once every 88 Earth days. The Earth's orbit takes one year, or 365 Earth days. There is a dwarf planet called Pluto, which is beyond the eight planets. Being farthest from the Sun, it has the longest journey: it takes a staggering 248 Earth years to complete one orbit!

AMAZING!

There could come a time when the Sun goes out! Scientists think that the Sun is running out of fuel. There is no need to panic though—this is happening very, very slowly. It probably still has enough fuel to keep on shining for more than five billion years.

THE SUN

THE SUN IS JUST A BIG BALL OF HOT AIR

The Sun is a star. And like all stars, it is a gigantic ball of burning gases. Hydrogen and helium are the two main gases that make up the fuel supply for the Sun's heat and light. The Sun has been burning for about five billion years and it will burn for at least that many more.

IT IS REALLY, REALLY HOT

Even the coolest part of the Sun, its surface, is 10,832 °F. This is 25 times hotter than the hottest kitchen oven. The Sun's center, or core, is many, many times hotter! The Sun is also enormously bright. In fact, its light, even though it comes from so far away, is strong enough to blind people.

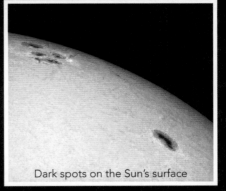
Dark spots on the Sun's surface

The Sun has spots bigger than planets

The Sun has little, slightly cooler pockets, which appear to be darker. Of course, these sunspots are "little" only when compared to the Sun—they can be as large as Jupiter. (Jupiter is the biggest planet in the solar system and is so big that all the other planets could fit inside it!)

There are times when the Sun hides

This happens at certain points of the Moon's orbit. In what is called an eclipse, the Moon comes between Earth and the Sun. The Sun is hidden behind the Moon, which casts a shadow across the surface of Earth.

AMAZING!

Dangerous ultraviolet (UV) rays from the Sun can burn your eyes and make you blind. This is why you must never, ever look directly at the Sun. Not even sunglasses can fully protect your eyes. If you want to see the Sun safely, ask someone to show you how to project its image onto a sheet of paper.

HAVE YOU EVER WONDERED . . .

HOW BIG IS EARTH WHEN COMPARED TO THE SUN?

Well, if the Sun were the size of a soccer ball, Earth wouldn't be much bigger than this period.

THE PLANETS

PLANETS WERE FORMED FROM WHIRLPOOLS OF GAS AND DUST

This happened about 4.6 billion years ago, inside a massive doughnut-shaped cloud of gas and dust that was spinning around the Sun. Some planets are still almost all gas, with no firm surface at all. Neither planets nor their moons are as big, or as hot, as stars, so they can't make light of their own.

Earth

Sun

Mercury

Venus

The eight planets of our solar system

AMAZING!

You can spot the brighter planets in the night sky even without a telescope. Venus shines white, while Jupiter looks greeny-blue, and Mars glows red. Of course, with a telescope you do get to see some amazing details.

(Left to right) The dwarf planets Pluto, Eris, Haumea, and Makemake

Neptune

Uranus

Jupiter

Saturn

Mars

SOME PLANETS ARE DWARFS

In 2006, the International Astronomical Union (IAU) downgraded Pluto to a dwarf planet. Although, like planets, it went around the Sun and was more or less ball-shaped, there was a difference: it had other similar-sized objects within its gravitational space. There are other dwarf planets: Makemake, Eris, and Haumea.

A planet is not a moon

A planet is a space body that orbits a star, for example, the Sun. A moon is a space body that orbits a planet. In the same way that planets are smaller than their star, moons are smaller than their planet.

HAVE YOU EVER WONDERED ...

HOW WERE PLANETS NAMED?

Most of the planets were given the names of ancient Roman gods by early astronomers a very long time ago.

THE MOONS

MOONS COME IN VARYING SHAPES AND SIZES

Most planets have moons—it is only Mercury and Venus that have no moons at all. Mars has two tiny, potato-shaped moons. Earth has one, which is nearly a hundred times wider than both of Mars's moons added together. Jupiter has 16, three of which are bigger than Earth's Moon.

Europa, one of Jupiter's moons, being observed by the spacecraft *Juno*, as it orbits the planet.

Moons do not make any light of their own

Earth's Moon works just like a big mirror, reflecting the Sun's light down towards us. Over the 29.3 days it takes to orbit Earth once, we get to see different amounts of its sunlit half. This is why it seems to change—from a crescent to a disk, and back again.

AMAZING!

You can be an incredible high-jumper on the Moon. The Moon's gravity is much weaker than Earth's. This means you would only weigh about a sixth of your Earth-weight there—and you'd be able to jump six times higher!

WHAT IS A HARVEST MOON?

It is the full, bright moon that occurs before the start of autumn. At one time, before the age of electricity, farmers relied on moonlight to harvest their crops late into the night—hence the name harvest moon.

The harvest moon hangs huge and bright in the night sky.

There is no life on our Moon

But there may be frozen water in rocks near its poles. The surface, which is a dusty, lifeless desert with no air or liquid water, is covered in wide, flat plains and high mountain ranges.

THE MOON'S SURFACE IS SCARRED WITH CRATERS

The Moon is 238,855 miles away. But, with a pair of good binoculars, it is possible to see the Moon's surface so clearly that you can make out individual craters, where huge space rocks have smashed into its surface.

Craters on the Moon's surface

THE EARTH

FROM SPACE, EARTH LOOKS LIKE A BEAUTIFUL, BLUE BALL

Earth, as seen from space

This color comes from the oceans that cover nearly three-quarters of our planet's surface. You can also see big patches of greeny-brown land and a swirling veil of white cloud. At night, when they are lit up with twinkling lights, it is even possible to make out cities.

Sunset in Santorini

As far as we know, Earth is the only planet in our solar system that has life

Over millions of years, as Earth cooled following the Big Bang, oceans formed and oxygen was made. Air, water, and the warmth of the Sun generated optimal conditions, and the first forms of life appeared and began to thrive.

AMAZING!

It's magnetic!

At the Earth's center is a core of a molten metal called iron, which means our planet acts as a giant magnet. Like all magnets, it has magnetic north and south poles. That is how a compass, which is also magnetic, indicates direction: its needle will always indicate where Earth's north lies, no matter where the compass is located.

Earth is just the perfect distance from the Sun

That is why there is life on our planet. If it were any closer, liquid water, which is a primary ingredient for life, would evaporate and we would sizzle and burn up in the heat. If it were farther away, we would have frozen to death.

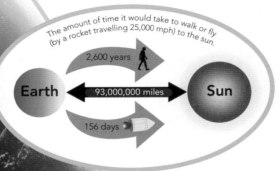

The amount of time it would take to walk or fly (by a rocket travelling 25,000 mph) to the sun.

2,600 years

Earth ← 93,000,000 miles → Sun

156 days

Day dawns on the region of Earth that spins into sunlight.

N

Night   Day   Sunlight

S

DAY AND NIGHT ARE FORMED BECAUSE THE EARTH SPINS

As it orbits the Sun, Earth, like all other planets, spins on its axis like a spinning top. When one part of the planet faces away from the Sun, it gets no light, and we say that night has fallen. At the same time, the opposite side, now facing the Sun, is in daylight.

HAVE YOU EVER WONDERED . . .

HOW OLD IS LIFE ON EARTH?

There has been life on Earth for approximately 3.5 billion years.

Algae were one of the earliest forms of life on Earth.

MERCURY AND VENUS

MERCURY IS THE SMALLEST PLANET IN THE SOLAR SYSTEM

It looks a lot like our Moon. About the same size, Mercury is similarly covered in craters, where pieces of space rock have crash-landed on its surface. Just like our Moon, it too has huge plains, rolling hills, deep gorges, chasms, and cliffs.

It's hot!

Though not the hottest planet, it certainly is scorching! Mercury has no air and hardly any atmosphere, which means there are no clouds to shield the surface of the planet from the baking-hot Sun during the day, or to keep in the heat at night. Nor does it have any wind or rain.

Mercury

When seen like this, it's clear how mu bigger Venus is in relation to Mercury

The surface of Mercury looks similar to Earth's Moon.

Venus rises in the evening sky.

Venus shines like a star

Despite being a planet, Venus is sometimes called the "evening star," because it is the first, and brightest, point of light to be seen shining in the sky as it gets dark. Of course, planets don't make their own light; Venus reflects the Sun's light in the same way that moons do.

Scientists believe there are ancient lava flows on Venus.

Venus

VENUS IS HOTTER

Venus is a searing 930°F—nearly 1.5 times hotter than Mercury, and over eight times hotter than the hottest place on Earth. This is because it's covered with thick clouds of heavy carbon dioxide, which act like a blanket, trapping the heat and keeping it in.

AMAZING!

Venus spins on its axis very slowly, so a day on that planet would stretch to 243 Earth days. On the other hand, it takes only 225 Earth days to go round the Sun once. Which means that one Venus day is longer than one Venus year!

HAVE YOU EVER WONDERED . . .

WHICH IS THE FASTEST PLANET IN THE SOLAR SYSTEM?

Mercury zips round the Sun at 106,993 mph in just 88 days, undisputedly winning that title.

MARS

MARS WAS NAMED AFTER THE ROMAN GOD OF WAR BECAUSE IT APPEARS TO BE RED—THE COLOR OF BLOOD

Mars and its moons, Deimos and Phobos

The color comes from the planet's rusty-red deserts of iron-rich soil and rock that cover most of its surface. Much like Earth, the planet has polar ice caps and clouds in its atmosphere, seasonal weather patterns, volcanoes, canyons, and other familiar natural features.

There may be liquid water on Mars

On Earth, where there is water, there is life. Spacecraft missions to Mars reveal that its south pole has a covering of dry ice (frozen carbon dioxide gas), below which there is water ice. On the other hand, water ice can be seen on the surface of Mars's north pole. Though liquid water has not yet been found, remains of freshwater lakes have been discovered.

AMAZING!

Mars's Olympus Mons is the solar system's biggest volcano. It is over 14.9 miles high—nearly three times higher than Mount Everest, the highest peak on Earth!

The red planet has a hazy pink sky with two moons

Mars's two tiny moons are named Deimos and Phobos. The two may have been asteroids (space rocks) that Mars captured with its gravity. Unlike our Moon, they are not round but look more like baked potatoes!

How Mars may have looked four billion years ago.

MARS AND EARTH WERE SIMILAR IN SOME WAYS BILLIONS OF YEARS AGO

While no evidence of life has been found on Mars, missions suggest that Mars had flowing rivers of water at some point in its history, so there could have been life. There may be fossilized remains of microscopic bacteria buried underground.

HAVE YOU EVER WONDERED . . .

What a human base on Mars might look like.

IS HUMAN HABITATION IN SPACE THE STUFF OF SCI-FI?

There are plans to send astronauts to Mars by the mid 2030s to check out whether space bases can be built there for scientists and explorers.

THE GAS GIANTS

IF A SPACECRAFT TRIED TO LAND ON THESE PLANETS, IT WOULD SINK BENEATH THE SURFACE!

This is because Jupiter, Saturn, Uranus, and Neptune are nothing but gas. They are all really large planets, but they do not have a solid surface.

Jupiter—the Great Red Spot is visible on the left edge of the image.

Each one of the giants is unique

Jupiter is so big that all the other planets in the solar system could squeeze inside it. It also spins so fast that a day and night on Jupiter last less than 10 Earth hours. More than 100 Earths would fit across Saturn's seven spectacular rings, but the planet is so light it would float on water. Neptune and Uranus have a distinct bluish-green color that is the result of the stinky gas methane contained in their atmospheres. Uranus has at least 27 moons—and those are just ones we know about!

26

HAVE YOU EVER WONDERED...

WHY DOES SATURN HAVE HULA-HOOP-LIKE RINGS?

In fact, all the gas giants have rings whirling around their middles. The rings of Jupiter and Neptune are mainly made of space dust, but the rings of Saturn and Uranus are chunkier, with lumps of ice and rock in them.

Uranus

SOMETHING ABOUT URANUS IS A LITTLE OUT OF SYNC

Uranus is tilted and travels around the Sun on its side. As a result, its poles are the warmest places on the planet, and summer at the south pole lasts 42 years!

Saturn

AMAZING!

There is a huge spinning storm on Jupiter that has been raging for 300 years! It covers an area that is large enough to fit two planet Earths. Clearly visible on the planet's surface, it is known as the Great Red Spot.

COLD, WINDY WORLDS

THERE IS NO COLDER WORLD THAN THIS

At almost 2.8 billion miles away from the Sun, Neptune is the eighth and outermost planet. Yet it is not the coldest planet. That honor belongs to Uranus, the seventh planet, which orbits the Sun at a distance of about 1.8 billion miles. The temperature on this frozen world is -371.2 °F.

PLUTO AND CHARON ARE OUR SOLAR SYSTEM'S ONLY DOUBLE-PLANETARY SYSTEM

Pluto has five moons, and the largest, Charon, is half Pluto's size. It is the only moon to be so big in relation to its parent body. The same surfaces of Charon and Pluto always face each other, a situation called mutual tidal locking. Charon orbits Pluto every 6.4 Earth days.

Charon

AMAZING!

While blocking some of the cold from reaching Neptune, Triton, the planet's ice-covered moon, bears the brunt of the freezing conditions. It records a low of -328 °F— just 122 °F short of being the lowest possible temperature in the entire Universe!

HAVE YOU EVER WONDERED ...

HOW SMALL COULD A DWARF PLANET BE?

At 1,473 miles across, Pluto is smaller than the United States or Russia!

Pluto

Four pictures of Neptune taken by the Hubble Space Telescope, four hours apart.

Pluto takes 248 Earth years to orbit the Sun once

This shows just how far the dwarf planet is from the Sun. Pluto's orbit has a funny shape, and for 20 years of its orbit it comes in closer to the Sun than Neptune, giving up its position as the farthest away from the Sun.

Winds rip across Neptune all the time

They blow at more than six times the speed of the most powerful hurricanes on Earth. Neptune's north and south poles, as well as the poles of its largest moon, Triton, are covered in frozen nitrogen, which looks like pink snow.

Triton

COMETS AND SHOOTING STARS

THERE ARE SNOWBALLS OUT THERE

Actually, comets only *look* like huge, dirty snowballs. Made of ice and rock dust, they are mostly found on the very edges of the solar system. Comets orbit the Sun just like planets do, but their paths are much more elongated. When a comet moves close enough to the Sun for the heat to bring its icy surface to a boil, the gases and dust stream out behind it, like a tail that stretches for many miles, away from the Sun.

SMALL ROCKY OBJECTS, SMALLER THAN PLANETS, ALSO ORBIT THE SUN

These bodies, called asteroids, tend to lurk in what is known as the main asteroid belt between Mars and Jupiter. But they can also be found in other locations around the solar system. Sometimes an asteroid crashes into another. The pieces that break off are called meteoroids.

Asteroids

A painting of the sighting of Halley's Comet in 1835

WHAT IT WOULD BE LIKE TO ACTUALLY SEE A COMET?

The most famous comet is Halley's Comet, which passes by and can be seen from Earth every 76 years. Measuring nine by five miles, it makes for a beautiful sight as it flies through the sky. The next time it will be visible from Earth is in 2061.

"Stars" can fall from the sky

Meteoroids enter Earth's atmosphere and break up into tiny, pea-sized pieces. They burn up into dust as they plunge through the air around Earth, looking like fireworks streaking across the night sky. That is why they are called shooting stars. The proper name for them is meteors.

One of the brightest meteors in the magical Perseid meteor shower was seen from an observatory in Chile.

AMAZING!

Sometimes many meteoroids enter Earth's atmosphere at the same time and can be seen as a meteor shower. Some showers happen at the same time every year, such as the Perseid meteor shower in August. Meteor showers can be fun to watch, so make a note of the date.

Comet Hale-Bopp streaks across the sky over Croatia.

WHEN STARS DIE

A white dwarf

There are many stars that are much bigger than our Sun—up to 1,000 times bigger, and with a lot more fuel. But, after burning for billions of years, eventually all stars run out of fuel. Generally speaking, the bigger the star, the shorter its life, and the faster it dies. The very biggest stars, the super giants, go out with a bang, in an explosion called a supernova.

Others become red giants

Not all stars make a lot of noise going out. There are some that, when they start to run out of fuel, swell up ... and grow ... and grow. Medium-sized stars like our Sun can become as much as 100 times bigger. These huge stars are called red giants.

A brightly burning giant star.

32

Red giants become white dwarfs

After a red giant uses up all its gas, it shrinks and can become as much as 10,000 times smaller. It is then a white dwarf. Despite being much smaller, the star still remains very hot.

The Crab nebula is a mass of dust and gas, left over from a supernova explosion.

The blue spot in the center of the red ring is a neutron star, in a neighboring galaxy.

THERE ARE ALSO THE "LITTLE GREEN MEN"

Deep in space are pulsars, the remains of supernovae. Known as "Little Green Men" (LGM), these are tiny but dense neutron stars that spin very fast. Some manage one rotation every four seconds, others whizz around a hundred times in a single second. As they spin, they pulse high-energy radio signals that are picked up by instruments on Earth.

AMAZING!

Today, special radio telescopes are used to "listen" for more pulsars. When astronomers in Cambridge, England, first spotted the pulsar LGM1, they wondered if it could be an alien distress beacon or some other kind of coded message!

HAVE YOU EVER WONDERED . . .

HOW MUCH LIGHT A SUPERNOVA WOULD GENERATE?

A supernova can be billions of times as bright as the Sun. It can outshine a whole galaxy.

BLACK HOLES, DARK MATTER

WHEN A REALLY HUGE STAR COLLAPSES AND DIES, THE AREA IT OCCUPIED IN SPACE FORMS A BIG BLACK HOLE

The force of gravity in a black hole is so strong that it sucks everything in. Nothing can escape the drag, not even light. And, because beams of light cannot escape, black holes hadn't ever been seen, not even with the most powerful telescope ever made. Until recently, that is. In 2019 the first image of a black hole was captured by a network of radio telescopes called the Event Horizon Telescope.

A black hole would suck you in like a whirlpool.

HAVE YOU EVER WONDERED . . .

HOW COULD YOU AVOID A BLACK HOLE?

You cannot see a black hole so it would be quite difficult to avoid one. Besides, if you went anywhere near it, you would be sucked inside, kind of like how water is sucked down a drain.

If something can't be seen, it doesn't mean that it isn't there

By watching and measuring how galaxies move, scientists are able to guess how much matter there is in the Universe. They can figure out that there is a lot more to the Universe than meets the eye! Stars and planets only make up a small part of the Universe.

The Abell 1689 galaxy cluster, where the presence of dark matter is believed to have been detected.

DARK MATTER IS ALL THE STUFF IN THE UNIVERSE SCIENTISTS KNOW MUST EXIST BUT ARE UNABLE TO FIND

It's super intriguing; more so because, even with no way of actually "seeing" dark matter, scientists may have been able to identify what it is made of. They think it might be made of tiny little ghostly particles called neutrinos.

The first-ever image of a black hole was revealed in 2019. It lies at the center of a galaxy called Messier 87.

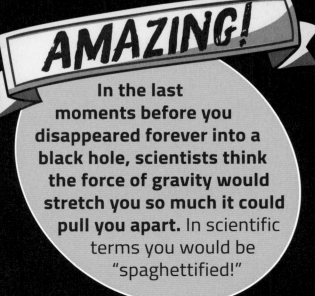

AMAZING!

In the last moments before you disappeared forever into a black hole, scientists think the force of gravity would stretch you so much it could pull you apart. In scientific terms you would be "spaghettified!"

35

OUR BLUE
PLANET

THIS IS OUR EARTH

EARTH IS MILLIONS AND MILLIONS OF YEARS OLD

Scientists think planet Earth was formed about 4.6 billion years ago. In the beginning, it was no more than a giant cloud of hot gas and dust. Over billions of years, this cloud shrank and cooled to form a huge ball, slightly squashed at the top and bottom.

It would be a long walk around the world.

AMAZING!

Earth weighs a whopping 13,170,000,000,000,000,000,000,000 lbs!

To walk around the middle of Earth, at the equator, where it is fattest, would take almost a year, provided you did not stop at all. At the end, you would have walked about 24,901 miles.

It is a ball made of four layers of metal and rock

The inner core at the center is a solid sphere of iron and nickel. Surrounding this is an outer core made up of liquid iron and nickel. A hot, viscous layer, a little like sticky caramel, made up of molten rock, wraps around the outer core. This is the mantle, and it is the thickest of the four layers. On the mantle floats the crust, the hard, rocky surface on which we live.

HAVE YOU EVER WONDERED . . .

WHAT IS THE CENTER OF EARTH LIKE?

It is incredibly hot deep inside Earth—about 8,132 °F. That's 20 times hotter than the hottest oven.

ONCE UPON A TIME, EARTH WAS UNFIT FOR ANY FORM OF LIFE

For the first billion years after the planet was formed, conditions were not suitable for life. Earth was a hostile place, extremely hot, with volcanoes spewing gases and lava. There were no plants or animals of any kind. Life began only about 3.8 billion years ago.

Volcanic activity is a reminder of the heat that simmers under Earth's crust.

THE ATMOSPHERE

THE ATMOSPHERE IS A THIN SKIN OF AIR THAT REACHES UP FOR ABOUT 300 MILES ABOVE THE SURFACE OF EARTH

It is made up of many gases, the more important ones being nitrogen and oxygen, and the atmosphere gets thinner as you travel farther away from Earth's surface. That's why mountaineers need to carry oxygen when they climb high peaks. Space begins where Earth's atmosphere ends.

AN OZONE LAYER IN THE ATMOSPHERE ACTS LIKE SUNSCREEN

Ozone gas forms a thin layer, 9-22 miles above the ground. It shields us from the harmful effects of the Sun's ultraviolet rays, which can damage the eyes, cause diseases such as skin cancer, and also severely affect plant life on Earth.

The ozone layer

STRATOSPHERE

OZONE LAYER

TROPOSPHERE

EARTH

The atmosphere protects Earth from burning up by blocking some of the Sun's rays.

A
5% Absorbed

Ozone hole over the South Pole caused by factories spewing smoke

CAN THE OZONE LAYER BE DAMAGED?

Yes, there are already holes in the ozone layer, due to the harmful effect of gases released by industry and other human activities. The main hole is above the South Pole. Scientists are working hard to contain and reduce the damage.

It affects climatic patterns as well as weather conditions. It also protects Earth from being hit by meteoroids, most of which burn up as they enter the atmosphere.

B
95% Absorbed

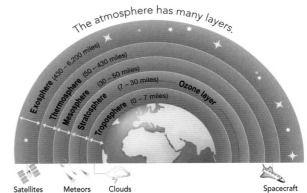

The atmosphere has many layers.

Exosphere (430 – 6,200 miles)
Thermosphere (50 – 430 miles)
Mesosphere (30 – 50 miles)
Stratosphere (7 – 30 miles)
Troposphere (0 – 7 miles)
Ozone layer

Satellites   Meteors   Clouds   Spacecraft

AMAZING!

As sunlight passes through the atmosphere, it breaks up and scatters. Some colors—violet, indigo, blue, and green—are scattered more than the others, and they mix together to turn the sky blue. At sunset or sunrise, when the Sun is low and sunlight has to travel farther through the atmosphere to reach us, yellow, orange, and red are scattered the most, resulting in a fiery orange sky.

THE GROUND BENEATH OUR FEET

OF ALL EARTH'S LAYERS, ONLY THE CRUST IS HOME TO LIFE

The surface of Earth, the crust, is formed of rocks and minerals, and varies in thickness. On dry land, it can be 25 miles thick. Under the seabed, it thins out in places to a mere five miles. It's an extraordinary thought that not a single life form has been found anywhere in the known Universe so far other than on and in Earth's crust.

Upper mantle

AMAZING!

Billions of years ago, before they drifted away into the positions we see them in today, all the continents were joined together as one big land mass. They still continue to drift almost 1.5 inches each year.

Crust

Inner core

Outer core

Lower mantle

The folds in hard rocks indicate the pressure under which they formed.

WHAT IS AT THE TOP AND BOTTOM OF EARTH?

Though Earth is round, the North and South Poles are said to lie at either end. The North Pole is surrounded by the frozen Arctic Ocean. The South Pole is in the middle of icy Antarctica. They are the coldest places on Earth.

EARTH'S CRUST IS BROKEN INTO PIECES KNOWN AS TECTONIC PLATES

The plates are visible as land masses and also exist under the oceans. The seven biggest are the African, Antarctic, Eurasian, North American, South American, Indo-Australian, and the Pacific plates. These, and other smaller plates, are always moving, floating very slowly on Earth's mantle. This movement formed the continents, oceans, and mountains, and also causes earthquakes and volcanic eruptions.

The rocks in Earth's crust are formed in different ways

Some rocks are pushed underground, where the heat and pressure transform them into metamorphic rock. Others, called igneous rocks, cool and harden after they shoot out of erupting volcanoes. Yet other rocks are formed when minerals and organic particles, such as sand grains or shells, are pressed down over time in layers. These are called sedimentary rocks.

A surface break in one of Earth's tectonic plates

RUMBLING EARTHQUAKES

Pressure pulls the crust in different directions, causing movement.

SOMETIMES TWO PIECES OF EARTH'S CRUST PUSH AGAINST EACH OTHER, CRASH TOGETHER, OR PULL APART, MAKING THE EARTH QUAKE

The plates that make up Earth's crust are constantly drifting on the molten rock beneath. This constant movement puts pressure on Earth's crust, causing cracks, called faults. The city of San Francisco in the USA sits on the San Andreas Fault, which is why it has hundreds of earthquakes a year.

A road in New Zealand, ripped open by an earthquake

Earthquake devastation

THE LONGEST EARTHQUAKE EVER RECORDED LASTED FOR FOUR MINUTES

However, most quakes last for less than a minute. Despite being fairly short-lived, earthquakes cause tremendous damage. Huge cracks open up in the ground. Houses, roads, and bridges shake and fall down. In the worst earthquakes, many people are injured and killed by buildings that collapse on them.

HOW SCIENTISTS MEASURE AN EARTHQUAKE?

Scientists measure the shock waves that ripple through the ground when an earthquake occurs, placing them on a scale of 1 to 10. Each point on the scale marks tremors 30 times worse than the one before.

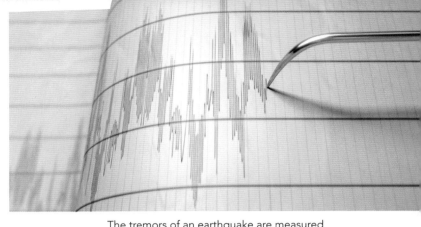

The tremors of an earthquake are measured by an instrument called a seismograph.

—Fault   Epicenter—   — Seismic waves

—Focus

How an earthquake happens

AMAZING!

When the Indian subcontinent crashed into the Asian continent, the force of the collision created the Himalayan mountain range, and some of the world's highest peaks. The Himalayas are still growing, pushed upwards by the subcontinent, which continues to drift north, pressing into Asia.

The tremors can be felt a long way away

The place where an earthquake begins is called the epicenter; it is where the ground trembles most violently. Stronger tremors at the epicenter push the impact of the earthquake over a wider area. The vibrations from an earthquake radiate outward with such force that they can be felt hundreds, even thousands, of miles away.

MYSTERIOUS CAVES

A cave like this could take thousands of years to form.

CAVES CAN BE AS BIG AS CATHEDRALS

There are many places all over the world where, over many thousands of years, huge chambers have been carved out underground. Some can be as large as cathedrals. When tunnels connect several chambers, it makes for an amazing subterranean system.

HAVE YOU EVER WONDERED...

WHAT ARE THE LONG, POINTED, ROCKY GROWTHS INSIDE CAVES?

They are called stalagmites and stalactites, and are formed by minerals deposited by dripping water. Stalactites stick tightly to the ceiling and grow downward. Stalagmites grow up from the floor, usually where drips from the ends of stalactites fall. Sometimes the two meet to form a column. The world's tallest stalagmite is 105 ft high. That's as tall as at least 18 people!

Icy stalagmites reach up from the floor of a cave system.

It takes many years to carve out even a small cave

When it rains, a weak acidic solution is formed, as the rain mixes with carbon dioxide in the atmosphere. This trickles through cracks in the ground, slowly eating away at the rocks. It could take as many as 100,000 years for this process to create a cave big enough for a human to fit in.

Caves carved out in cliffs by water

CAVES CAN BE FORMED BY LAVA, ICE, AND WAVES

Interesting systems are formed in a variety of ways: for example, when the outer surface of an underground lava flow cools and hardens, the molten rock inside flows away, leaving behind a tube-like cave. In icy glaciers, melting water carves out tunnels and caves as it begins to flow. Cliffs at the edge of coastlines can be dotted with caves where waves have cut into them.

Exploring a cave system

AMAZING!

Spelunkers are people who like to explore caves and tunnels. They climb down ropes or ladders into the dark, wet and cold underground. Sometimes these caves may be underwater, or barely large enough for a person to squeeze through.

TOWERING MOUNTAINS

A MOUNTAIN MUST BE AT LEAST 1,000 FT TALL

Geologists, the people who study Earth and what it's made of, say that for a landform to be classified as a mountain it must be at least 1,000 feet higher than its surrounding landscape. A mountain usually has steep slopes, and the highest point of a mountain is called the peak, or summit. Hills are smaller and less steep. A series, or chain, of mountains that cluster close together, is known as a mountain range.

Parkhouse Hill in England is tiny compared with Mount Everest!

Formation of block mountains
A raised block is called a horst and a depressed valley a graben.

Mount Everest, in the Himalayas

WHY ARE SOME MOUNTAINTOPS ALWAYS SNOWY?

The higher you climb up a mountain, the thinner the air gets. The atmosphere changes from a snug blanket of protection to a very loosely woven one, and its ability to absorb and retain the warmth of the Sun decreases. So, at the top of a high mountain, it's freezing cold, and the ice and the snow never melt.

AMAZING!

The tallest mountain, measured from top to bottom, is Mauna Kea, an inactive volcano on the island of Hawaii in the Pacific Ocean. Mauna Kea stands 33,474 ft tall, though it rises only 13,796 ft above the sea. The summit of Mount Everest, at 29,035 ft, is the highest point on Earth.

IT TAKES A GREAT DEAL OF FORCE TO PUSH UP A MOUNTAIN

Mountains can be formed in various ways. When pieces of Earth's crust crash into each other, they squash the rock into giant folds. Mountains formed like this, such as the Himalayas, are the tallest in the world. Sometimes, the pressure of two plates pushing against each other forces huge chunks of rock up and down to form block mountains. When the plates keep pushing steadily for a long time, the crust forms a dome or plateau, which is not as high. When molten rock from deep inside Earth bursts out through the crust and piles up on itself, it forms what are known as volcanic mountains.

49

FIERY VOLCANOES

DEEP UNDER EARTH, THERE IS RED-HOT, RUNNY, MOLTEN ROCK CALLED MAGMA

When magma discovers an opening in Earth's surface, it either bursts out in a spectacular eruption, throwing burning ash, gas, and liquid rock high up into the air; or it oozes out as rivers of lava. (Lava is the name given to magma when it reaches Earth's surface.) As it cools, lava turns into hard, black rock.

Every continent has volcanoes

There are volcanoes all over the world—even in the biting cold of Antarctica! Most volcanoes are formed along the boundaries of the tectonic plates. As they shift continually, grinding, bumping, and crashing into each other, they create weak points where magma can erupt.

AMAZING!

Almost 75 percent of the world's active volcanoes are located in the "Ring of Fire." This 25,854-mile-long, horseshoe-shaped zone covers a large area from the southern tip of South America, up to the west coast of North America, then through the Bering Sea to Japan and down to New Zealand.

SOME VOLCANOES ARE SLEEPING

Volcanoes can be active, dormant, or extinct. Active volcanoes have erupted recently, or are expected to erupt in the near future. Extinct volcanoes are those that last erupted a very long time ago and are not expected to erupt again—although they could surprise us. Dormant is the name given to volcanoes when no one is really sure what their status is! They no longer erupt, but they may just be sleeping and could erupt again sometime in the future.

Mount St. Helens volcano, Washington State, USA

The Tungurahua volcano in Ecuador erupting

HAVE YOU EVER WONDERED...

WHY DO PEOPLE CHOOSE TO LIVE NEAR VOLCANOES?

Many people live near volcanoes even though it's dangerous. The ash that shoots out of a volcano makes the soil very rich and perfect for growing crops.

A village near the Merapi volcano in Indonesia

ICEBERGS AND GLACIERS

GLACIERS ARE ENORMOUS RIVERS OF ICE

They form in the higher reaches of mountains when snow collects in dips in the rock. As the snow piles up, it hardens and turns to ice, which then begins to slide downhill, usually no more than a few inches a day.

HAVE YOU EVER WONDERED . . .

WHAT IF A SHIP COLLIDED WITH AN ICEBERG?

Icebergs are very dangerous to passing ships and boats. In 1912 the luxury liner *Titanic* hit an iceberg on its maiden (first-ever) voyage, from Southampton to New York, and sank in the North Atlantic Ocean.

The cracked surface of the Skaftafellsjökull glacier, Iceland

An iceberg in the North Atlantic Ocean

Some glaciers cover the ground like a bed sheet

Another kind of glacier is called an ice sheet. These spread outward from the center in all directions, covering everything. Antarctica and the island of Greenland are covered with ice sheets.

Some glaciers flow directly into the sea, where the large chunks that break away float off as icebergs.

ICEBERGS ARE BROKEN PIECES OF GLACIERS

When a glacier meets the sea, the front of it lifts and floats in water. The sheer cliff that it forms could be as tall as 197 ft. Every now and then, giant chunks of ice break off the ends of glaciers and drift out to sea. This is called "calving," and these chunks of ice are called icebergs. Smaller icebergs are called "bergy bits."

Glaciers may be slow but they are very powerful

Glaciers push ahead like bulldozers, carrying with them any rocks and stones they may bump into, and scraping away at the rocks on the side. They carve out deep valleys along the way. Different parts of a glacier move at different speeds. As the base of the glacier grinds against the ground, it slows down, while the ice higher up can flow much faster.

AMAZING!

Only about a tenth of an iceberg shows above water. The rest is hidden under the sea.

53

TUMBLING RIVERS

Rocks and stones on the banks of a young river

MOST RIVERS BEGIN AS SMALL FAST-FLOWING STREAMS HIGH UP ON MOUNTAINSIDES

They may flow from lakes, or trickle from the tips of an icy glacier as it starts to melt. Some rivers start off as springs bubbling up out of the ground. The place where a river starts is called its source.

The Li River, as it meanders through the hills of Guangxi Province, China

AMAZING!

The Nile in Egypt, which flows for 4,347 miles, is the longest river on Earth. However, the Amazon in South America, which is only 183 miles shorter, is the biggest river, carrying 60 times more water than the Nile. D River in Oregon, USA, is the world's shortest river, measuring just 120 ft, which is roughly 180,000 times shorter than the Nile!

Young rivers are very powerful

As a river tumbles downhill from its source, the force of the water tears away at its edges, pulling out rocks and stones. These roll along with the water, carving out deep valleys and gorges.

The Nile

People have settled and built cities on riverbanks from the earliest times

Rivers carry a lot of soil and silt down mountains. Away from the mountains, rivers flow slowly, spreading out over flatter ground. Losing momentum, they deposit the debris on the riverbed, as well as the surrounding plains during floods. This fertile soil is ideal for farming, which is why people have always settled along riverbanks.

HAVE YOU EVER WONDERED . . .

ARE THERE RIVERS UNDERGROUND?

As rainwater trickles underground, it can sometimes form rivers that flow through caves and tunnels. However, very few people have ever seen them.

A LOT OF WATER IN RIVERS IS RECYCLED

Rivers form an essential link in the water cycle. The heat of the Sun causes millions of gallons of sea water to evaporate and turn into invisible water vapor. This rises into the atmosphere and cools to form clouds. Clouds drift over the land and rain down on it. Rainwater flows into the rivers, which carry it back to the ocean, where it evaporates once more.

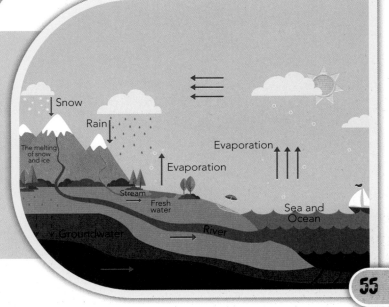

Snow

Rain

The melting of snow and ice

Stream

Fresh water

Groundwater

River

Evaporation

Evaporation

Sea and Ocean

HOW
LIFE BEGAN

IN THE BEGINNING

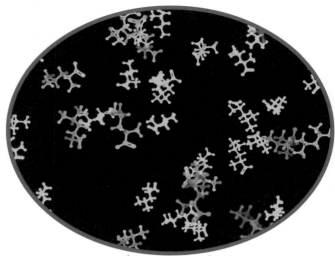
Amino acid strands

ONCE UPON A TIME, THERE WAS NO LIFE ON EARTH

For the first 1,000 million years after Earth came into existence, there were no plants or animals of any kind. Earth was an inhospitable place where life could not survive.

HAVE YOU EVER WONDERED . . .

HOW LONG AGO WAS IT THAT LIFE APPEARED ON EARTH?

The first-known living things appeared in the oceans about 3.5 billion years ago. It is possible that life may have begun earlier, but scientists haven't been able to prove that.

AMAZING!

Life was born into a world that looked very different. If you could travel back, you would think it was an alien planet. The sky was pink; the sea rusty-red; and the atmosphere was filled with poisonous gases.

Life first appeared in the ocean

Scientists have put forward the theory that life was jolted into existence when a huge bolt of lightning struck the sea. Chemicals that existed in the sea reacted to this burst of energy and mixed together to create new substances called amino acids. Life grew from these amino acids.

Stromatolites

A bolt of lightning may have triggered life.

IT BEGAN WITH BACTERIA

The first living things were microscopically tiny bacteria. Each one was a single living unit called a cell, and hundreds of them would have fit on a point as tiny as a pinhead. Sometimes, layer upon layer of these tiny cells built up in shallow water, creating big mounds that scientists call stromatolites.

Then came algae

Slowly some bacteria changed into algae, which were simple plants. Algae lived in the sea in masses, like huge blankets. They made oxygen, which helped to turn the sky and sea blue.

Life began in water.

THE FIRST FORMS OF LIFE

THE FIRST LIVING CREATURES HAD NO BONES

Life on Earth evolved very slowly. The first-known multicelled sea creatures didn't appear until about 800 million years ago. They looked a little like worms and jellyfish, and had no bones or shells.

The first multicellular life forms may have looked like this.

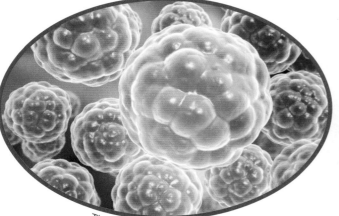

An illustration of some prehistoric plants

PLANTS EVOLVED ON LAND BEFORE ANIMALS

About 440 million years ago, the first life on land appeared as simple plants that looked very much like today's mosses. The first proper plant with roots and a stem was *Cooksonia*, from about 420 million years ago. Then, about 400 million years ago, came the first land animals—worms, spiders, scorpions, and insects.

Anomalocaris: a large, shrimp-like predator that lived in water and measured about one yard in length.

Sea animals grew shells and spines for protection

The first-known sea animals with armor-like shells began to appear about 550 million years ago. The shells helped protect their soft bodies from attack by enemies. It was also about this time that some sea animals developed legs.

Dragonflies, many times bigger than this modern descendant, were the first animals to fly.

Fish were the first to develop backbones

By 500 million years ago, fish had appeared in the oceans. As they evolved, they became the first animals to develop a proper backbone, but they had no fins yet, and looked kind of like tadpoles. Some of them also grew lungs, which meant they could breathe air and live in water and on land.

AMAZING!

Insects were the first animals to fly. The first in the air were giant dragonflies, like *Meganeura*. By 300 million years ago, there were dragonflies the size of kites. Some early creatures were longer than your arm—imagine meeting millipedes twice as long as a bicycle!

HAVE YOU EVER WONDERED . . .

HOW ANIMALS GREW LEGS?

Some of the first fish began to live in shallow water, where it was difficult to swim. They grew short legs to help them move as they evolved to adapt to their environment.

BOTH ON LAND AND IN WATER

The skeleton of an Acanthostega

ANIMALS APPEARED WITH A "DOUBLE LIFE"

The word "amphibian" means "double life" in Greek. It's easy to see why it was chosen as a label for animals that can live on land as well as in water. The development of amphibians marked a milestone in the complexity of life forms on land. Up to then, life on land consisted of millions of insects and worms that were supported by simple plants.

AMAZING!

As they started moving around outside the water, amphibians discovered plentiful new food sources. Even better, they faced fewer predators on land. Soon, amphibians were taking over the land to the extent that this period is called the "Age of the Amphibian."

The amphibious Ichthyostega

Walking fish

Animals with backbones such as *Ichthyostega* and *Acanthostega*, ancestors of the amphibians, appeared on Earth about 350 million years ago. They evolved from fish whose fins had become legs. They could crawl onto land but still had gills that allowed them to breathe underwater.

The jelly-like eggs of a frog

THESE ANIMALS STILL NEEDED TO STAY CLOSE TO WATER

Though they could survive on land, there were many reasons why the first amphibians did not venture very far from water. Their skin was still very soft and needed to be kept damp. The amphibians' eggs were jelly-like and needed to be laid in water to stop them from drying out. The young also needed to stay in the water until they lost their gills and developed lungs.

HAVE YOU EVER WONDERED...

DO AMPHIBIANS STILL EXIST?

There are many different amphibians in the world today. For example, frogs, toads, and salamanders are all amphibians.

Today's amphibians still look similar to their ancestors.

LIZARD-LIKE REPTILES

BY ABOUT 300 MILLION YEARS AGO, A NEW ANIMAL GROUP HAD EVOLVED

These were reptiles. Not only could they live on land all the time, but they could also live away from water. Their skin had become dry and scaly, and their eggs were protected from drying out by a leathery shell. The small, lizard-like *Hylonomus* was one of the first.

Sarcosuchus

Hylonomus

Reptiles had to learn how to run quickly

The chameleon has to be quicker than the beetle to make it a meal.

By the time reptiles evolved, Earth was already populated with insects, which ensured plentiful food. But insects were fast runners, and reptiles had to learn to move quickly so they could catch their next meal. As the reptiles became larger, they hunted and ate bigger prey, including other reptiles. There were also some who stuck to eating only plants.

There's a good reason why today's crocodiles look a lot like early reptiles: **they've evolved from them.** Scientists think that *Sarcosuchus*, one of the crocodile's early ancestors, grew to a massive 36–39 ft—three times as long as today's biggest crocodiles!

HAVE YOU EVER WONDERED ...

HOW DID DINOSAURS EVOLVE?

Early reptiles like *Chasmatosaurus* walked on all fours, but over time some reptiles raised themselves up and began to walk on their back legs. After these speedy, two-legged reptiles like the *Lagosuchus* came the dinosaurs.

Lagosuchus

SOME REPTILES CARRIED "SAILS" ON THEIR BACKS

Reptiles were cold-blooded, which means their bodies relied on the Sun's heat to warm them. Scientists think the sail-like fins on the backs of reptiles, like those on the *Dimetrodon*, worked like solar panels, soaking up heat. It is possible that the fins could lose heat as well, in order to regulate body temperature. Some prehistoric reptiles grew fur on their bodies to keep themselves warm. These would go on to evolve into mammals.

A *Dimetrodon* skeleton

THE AGE OF DINOSAURS

MORE THAN 800 KINDS OF DINOSAURS HAVE BEEN NAMED

Dinosaurs came in many amazing shapes and sizes. Scientists have named about 880 types, but there were many more. They evolved from a group called the "ruling reptiles," which appeared about 250 million years ago—about 20 million years before the first dinosaurs. Some scientists think *Lagosuchus* (which means rabbit crocodile) was the ancestor of all dinosaurs.

Brachiosaurus was a sauropod dinosaur, one of the largest and most popular. It lived during the Late Jurassic period.

HAVE YOU EVER WONDERED ...

WHERE IN THE WORLD DID DINOSAURS LIVE?

Everywhere, but the planet was completely different in dinosaur times. The seas, plants, animals, and continents were all different. And there were no people!

AMAZING!

Many scientists believe that 65 million years ago, a gigantic chunk of space rock smashed into the Earth. It threw up huge clouds of dust, which blocked out the Sun. Plunged into freezing darkness, plants couldn't grow, and plant-eating dinosaurs died of cold and hunger. In turn, without their plant-eating prey, meat-eaters starved to death.

Spinosaurus had a "sail-back" and lived in Africa.

Fossilized dinosaur eggs

Dinosaurs ruled the world for millions of years

These huge reptiles appeared about 230 million years ago, and died out 65 million years ago. There were three periods in dinosaur history: Triassic, when the first dinosaurs appeared; and Jurassic and Cretaceous, when dinosaurs dominated the land. They were adapted for life on land, and the fact that they walked with straight legs tucked underneath their bodies, like humans do, gave them an advantage over other animals.

FOSSILIZED DINOSAUR EGGS HAVE BEEN FOUND IN MANY PLACES

These huge creatures laid eggs, just like reptiles and birds do today. The eggs were only about five inches long. Had they been bigger, the shell would have been too thick for the young to break through. Fossil eggs have been found all over the world. Most are empty, but some eggs have the fossilized bones of baby dinosaurs inside.

A small mammal keeps its eyes on three *Parasaurolophus* as they meander along the water's edge.

DINOSAURS OF ALL SHAPES AND SIZES

THESE WERE THE LARGEST ANIMALS TO EVER WALK ON EARTH

In the Jurassic age, giant plant-eaters called sauropods became the largest animals to ever walk on Earth. One of them, *Ultrasaurus*, may have measured 98 ft long and about 59 ft high, which is as tall as a six-story building! *Brachiosaurus* was also massive. Measuring more than 72 ft from head to tail, this dinosaur was about as long as a tennis court and heavier than five elephants. It was tall enough to peer over the top of a four-story house!

Imagine a face-off between a plant-eating *Brachiosaurus* and a *Tyrannosaurus rex*!

AMAZING!

***Tyrannosaurus* means "tyrant lizard."**

When scientists chose the word "rex"—Latin for "king"—it was because *T. rex* was big and mean enough to rule over all the rest: killing and eating anything it wanted. But *Giganotosaurus*, meaning "giant southern lizard," was another meat-eater that was even bigger than *Tyrannosaurus!*

Dinosaurs ate everything—even each other

Meat-eaters such as *Allosaurus* had strong claws to grip their victims, powerful jaws and long, curved, dagger-like teeth to kill and tear prey. *Carcharodontosaurus* had a huge skull, five feet across, and jaws full of shark-like teeth. *Yunnanosaurus* had chisel-shaped teeth to cut up tough vegetation. Diplodocids could strip branches in seconds with teeth that looked like pencils. Plant-eaters swallowed stones called gastroliths, to help grind down tough plant matter inside their stomachs.

Two *Allosaurus* on the prowl

HAVE YOU EVER WONDERED . . .

WERE ALL DINOSAURS BIG?

Some dinosaurs were tiny. *Compsognathus* wasn't much larger than a turkey! It hunted insects and lizards. *Heterodontosaurus* and *Lesothosaurus*, both plant-eating dinosaurs, were just as small.

SCIENTISTS HAVE NO IDEA WHAT COLOR DINOSAURS WERE

No one has found a fossil that shows what color any of the dinosaurs were. Scientists think that some were brightly colored, while others were patterned to match their surroundings—just like many animals are today. There is also no way of knowing what noises they made or how they behaved.

REPTILES IN THE WATER

Mosasaurus

SOME REPTILES WENT BACK TO THE WATER

At the time when dinosaurs ruled the land, a number of strange reptiles swam in the seas. There were three main groups: sea turtles, ichthyosaurs, and the long-necked plesiosaurs. Sea reptiles had to surface to breathe air, just like dolphins and whales do today.

Ichthyosaurus

SOME SEA REPTILES LOOKED LIKE FISH

Ichthyosaurs were strong swimming reptiles that looked very much like today's dolphins, and they could breathe air. They probably hunted in packs, feeding on fish and squid. Fossils found indicate that ichthyosaurs actually gave birth to live young.

Mosasaurus was a real sea monster and the largest lizard there has ever been. Measuring 32 ft, with a huge mouth, *Mosasaurus* looked like a dragon. It probably ate anything it could catch.

Fossils of sea turtles show they were enormous

The fossil specimen of an *Archelon* skeleton found in 1970 was more than 13 ft long and 16 ft wide—bigger than a rowboat. It looked a lot like a present-day leatherback sea turtle, with a narrow skull and pointed tail. Scientists think it ate jellyfish.

Archelon

Elasmosaurus

HAVE YOU EVER WONDERED . . .

Plesiosaurs had four paddle-like limbs and a tail

Plesiosaurs were also swimming reptiles. *Elasmosaurus*'s tiny head sat on an amazingly long neck that was half its total length of 42 ft. *Liopleurodon* was a short-necked plesiosaur, but its head was almost three feet long. It probably fed on shellfish and turtles, crunching them up with dagger-like teeth that were four inches long.

DO THE BIG SEA REPTILES STILL EXIST?

No. They all died out approximately 65 million years ago, at the same time as the dinosaurs.

WINGED REPTILES AND DINOBIRDS

FLYING REPTILES LOOKED A LOT LIKE BATS

At about the same time as the first dinosaurs appeared, some reptiles evolved wings. These flying reptiles were pterosaurs, not dinosaurs. Most had furry bodies and leathery wings that were flaps of skin. The biggest pterosaur of all was *Quetzalcoatlus*. Scientists think its outspread wings measured a whopping 50 ft, the biggest wingspan the world has ever known!

Quetzalcoatlus was a predator but also scavenged.

Pterodaustro

HAVE YOU EVER WONDERED . . .

ARE TODAY'S BIRDS RELATED TO PTEROSAURS OR DINOSAURS?

Pterosaurs became extinct about 65 million years ago, at the same time as the big sea reptiles. The birds that fly our skies today have evolved from dinosaurs. The next time you look at a bird, think of your favorite dinosaur!

Pterosaurs could attack baby dinosaurs

Some pterosaurs snapped up insects, while others dove down to the sea to catch fish. *Pterodaustro* probably sieved tiny sea creatures through the bristly teeth in its lower jaw, in the same way that flamingos do today. *Dsungaripterus* may have used the tip of its curved beak to pry shellfish off rocks. It's possible that *Quetzalcoatlus* could have carried away baby dinosaurs.

Archaeopteryx, the first true bird

IT'S POSSIBLE THAT THE FIRST BIRDS COULD NOT FLY

Birds evolved from small, meat-eating dinosaurs. Fossils of "dinobirds" found in China clearly show dinosaurs with feathers. The feathered dinosaur known as *Archaeopteryx*, which means "ancient wing," is accepted as the first true bird—a bird that could fly—though researchers still argue about whether it could flap its wings or whether it merely glided through the air.

AMAZING!

Today's hoatzin bird, which inhabits South America, has claws on its wings when young—just like *Archaeopteryx*, its prehistoric ancestor, did. There's also a lizard that can glide on wing-like flaps of skin, like the gliding reptiles of prehistoric times.

A pair of hoatzin

THE WARM-BLOODED MAMMALS

Megazostrodon

MAMMALS SURVIVED THE MASS EXTINCTION EVENT

The first mammals evolved from reptiles about 220 million years ago and shared the land with dinosaurs. They were not very big, though—*Megazostrodon*, one of the earliest, was barely bigger than a mouse. When dinosaurs died out, mammals not only survived but actually took over Earth. There are about 4,200 different kinds of mammals alive today.

Indricotherium

HAVE YOU EVER WONDERED . . .

WHICH WAS THE LARGEST LAND MAMMAL?

Indricotherium, the largest land mammal, was an early kind of rhinoceros. It was as heavy as four elephants and, at 26 feet in height, it was 1.5 times taller than a modern giraffe.

Mammals are warm-blooded, and their babies drink milk

Unlike amphibians, fish, and reptiles, mammals make their own body heat. They are also unique in that young mammals feed on milk produced by their mothers. Although the first mammal mothers laid eggs rather than giving birth to live young, this changed over time, with new kinds of mammal. Australia's duck-billed platypus is the best-known, egg-laying mammal still found today.

Duck-billed platypus

AMAZING!

When the first elephants appeared about 40 million years ago, they were tiny. *Moeritherium*, for example, was only about 24 inches high. All sorts of strange-looking variations evolved before the ancestors of modern elephants appeared about five million years ago.

THERE ARE MAMMALS THAT CAN SWIM, AND SOME THAT FLY

Bats are still the only mammals that can flap their wings to fly. *Icaronycteris*, the earliest-known bat, which lived about 54 million years ago, had a long tail. Whales, dolphins, and seals are mammals that developed ways of living in water. The earliest-known whale, *Pakicetus*, appeared at about the same time as the bats, and it looked more like a seal than a modern whale.

Icaronycteris

Moeritherium

FIRST CIVILISATIONS

THE FIRST PEOPLE

Early humans ate meat, leaves, fruit, and berries

The meat probably came from dead animals that they found, though they may also have hunted for some small animals. Plants gave them berries and leaves. They used stone tools to cut and scrape their food.

HUMAN LIFE FIRST BEGAN IN AFRICA

The earliest human-like creatures were the australopithecines, who were evolving as long as 4.5 million years ago. They were based in what is today eastern Africa, around Ethiopia, Kenya, and Tanzania. Being well adapted to live both in trees and on the ground, the australopithecines survived for almost a million years.

Australopithecus

HAVE YOU EVER WONDERED . . .

WHO WERE THE FIRST MUSICIANS?

No one knows when music began, but the world's oldest musical instrument is a whistle, carved from an animal bone, more than 60,000 years ago!

This flute made of bone is one of the earliest musical instruments—possibly 40,000 years old.

Early stone tools

The "handy man" began using tools

About two million years ago, *Homo habilis* appeared in eastern and southern Africa. About 39-53 inches tall and weighing approximately 70 pounds, *Homo habilis*, or "handy man," was the first tool user. He made simple tools, such as choppers, from stone.

Australopithecine skull fossil

AMAZING!

Scientists have been able to dig out the bones of more than 300 australopithecines. These, and other fossils, tell us that australopithecines had a flat nose, a strong lower jaw that stuck out, and small canine teeth. They stood and walked on two legs.

Models of *Homo erectus* displayed in the Vienna Museum of Natural History

HOMO ERECTUS, THE "UPRIGHT MAN," WAS A WANDERER

He appeared more than one million years ago. He was taller and heavier than *Homo habilis*, with longer legs and shorter arms, which indicate that he spent more time on the ground than climbing trees. It was *Homo erectus* who began moving out of Africa into Europe and Asia.

OUR NEANDERTHAL COUSINS

NEANDERTHALS WERE OUR CLOSEST HUMAN RELATIVES

A kind of early human, Neanderthals evolved several thousand years before *Homo sapiens*, the ancestor of modern humans. Neanderthals lived in Europe, and across southwestern and central Asia, between 400,000 and 40,000 years ago. This was during the Ice Age, when much of Earth was covered in ice and snow. No one really knows why they died out about 30,000 years ago.

HAVE YOU EVER WONDERED . . .

WHAT KIND OF ANIMALS DID NEANDERTHALS HUNT?

Huge mammoths and large hoofed animals were a major source of essential food, skins, and fur. Neanderthals had to invent clever ways of hunting, such as chasing animals over cliffs with burning branches, and then using spears to stab the injured prey to death.

Hunting a woolly mammoth

Painting of a Neanderthal family

By studying the marks of muscles on fossilized bones, scientists can tell that Neanderthals must have been very strong. It is also clear that they suffered many broken bones, perhaps because they hunted large animals close up. The fact that the bones had been broken at different times, and that they had healed well, indicates that injured members of the group were fed and taken care of properly.

Neanderthals did not look like our ancestors

A Neanderthal adult male's face reconstructed from the 40,000-year-old remains found in Belgium

They were a species quite distinct from *Homo sapiens*. Sturdier, with thick, strong bones, they were about 61–64.5 inches tall and weighed 121–143 pounds. The shape of their heads was different—the middle part of the face was broader with a large nose. However, their brains were the same size as ours.

THEY WERE SMART AND SKILFUL

Most researchers believe that Neanderthals used many tools and weapons, controlled fire, and were good hunters and skilled craftsmen—their hands were very much like ours. They lived in shelters, in groups of 10 to 15, took care of those hurt or sick, and buried their dead.

A Neanderthal cave shelter

THE APPEARANCE OF *HOMO SAPIENS*

Australopithecus

Neanderthalensis

Homo erectus

Homo sapiens

ALL PEOPLE ON EARTH TODAY ARE *HOMO SAPIENS*

The scientific name for modern humans is *Homo sapiens*, which means "wise man." Our ancestors, the first modern humans, first appeared in Africa about 180,000 years ago. From there, they spread out across the world.

A memorial built for the Iceman near the exact spot where he was discovered

How modern humans evolved

Modern humans started setting up the first homes

They lived in cave entrances, and in places sheltered by overhanging rocks. In the open, they made huts from branches covered with skins. They were mostly hunter-gatherers, meaning they lived on meat that they hunted and plant produce that they gathered.

AMAZING!

In 1991 a mummified body complete with clothes, weapons and even a backpack, was discovered frozen in the ice of the Alps. The mummy was nicknamed the Iceman, and it's one of the oldest ever found. When he died about 5,300 years ago, the Iceman was wearing a leather tunic and shoes, a furry hat, and a woven grass cape.

Homo sapiens evolved lighter skeletons than earlier humans

They also had much larger brains, which gave the skull a very different shape—with a higher, more vertical, forehead. The jaws of modern humans are also lighter, and the teeth are smaller.

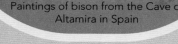

Paintings of bison from the Cave of Altamira in Spain

THEY WERE PAINTERS AND SCULPTORS

In Europe, modern humans were alive during the freezing Ice Age, a time when glaciers covered the land. They were among the first artists, painting pictures of horses, bison, and deer on the walls of their caves. Bone and ivory were carved into figures of animals and people.

HAVE YOU EVER WONDERED...

ARE THERE PREHISTORIC SECRETS HIDDEN BEHIND SHEETS OF ICE?

Freeze-dried mummies of many different animals—woolly mammoths, woolly rhinos, cave lions—have been discovered under the ice in the cold northlands of Siberia. In 2018 a mummified puppy was discovered, and in 2019 scientists found a perfectly preserved mummy of a two-month-old foal.

Mummified remains have been discovered in the frozen Siberian landscape.

CRAFTSMEN OF THE STONE AGE

THE FIRST TOOL WAS A SIMPLE ROCK

It was probably well over two million years ago that someone picked up a rock and made a stone tool from it. This event is considered the beginning of the Stone Age, which covers a very long period of time, right up to about 5,000 years ago, when bronze tools were first made.

WHY THE FIRST FIRES WERE TAKEN FROM THE WILD?

Experts think that it was *Homo erectus* who first tamed, and learned to control, fire, perhaps as far back as 1.6 million years ago. The first fire makers probably took flames from bush fires started by a flash of lightning.

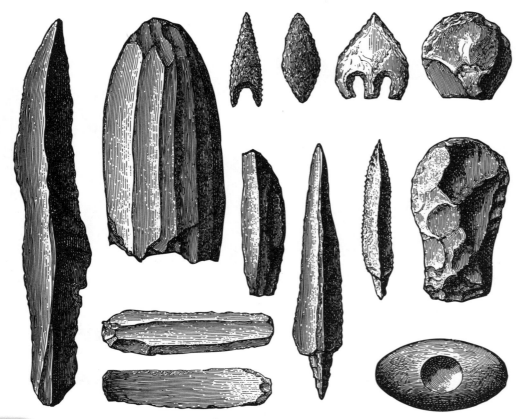

A variety of stone tools used by early humans

Homo erectus used chipped stones as sharp hand-axes

These were very useful for skinning animals and cutting up the meat. But not all Stone Age tools were made of stone. Later in the Stone Age, people made tools from animal bones, antlers, and ivory.

A fire-hardened spear

A hand ax

AMAZING!

About 30,000 years ago, our ancestors began to carve and paint pictures on cave walls and roofs. Most pictures were of the animals they hunted—charging bison, or a herd of leaping deer. Different kinds of earth provided yellow, red, and brown colors. White came from clay or chalky stones, while charcoal from burned twigs was the source for black. These people painted with their fingers, as well as making brushes by attaching animal fur to sticks. Sometimes, they spray-painted by blowing paint through a hollow bone.

THE EARLIEST WEAPONS WERE POINTED, WOODEN STICKS USED AS HUNTING SPEARS

It is likely that *Homo erectus* first made them, more than 400,000 years ago. Much later, about 25,000 years ago, an innovative early human sharpened bone into sewing needles and started a whole new fashion!

A bison hunt drawn on a rock

THE FIRST FARMERS

Llamas were domesticated by ancient farmers.

THE FIRST CROP HARVESTED WAS GRAIN FROM WILD GRASSES

Hunter-gatherers had to move from place to place in search of food. Things began to change about 10,000 years ago when people in the Middle East began to collect and store grain they found growing wild. They also realized that, if they scattered some of the wild seeds on the soil around their huts, they could grow their own crops. Now that there was no need to go in search of food, they could settle down in more permanent homes.

Maize and sweet potatoes were two of the first crops.

The domestic Saarloos dog-wolf of today is closely related to wild wolves.

AMAZING!

People had begun domesticating animals even before they settled down. Gradually, wolves began to live and hunt alongside humans, and followed them as they moved around. Fed and petted, the wolf was the first animal to be domesticated, and its descendant, the dog, is now known as "man's best friend!"

Taming wild animals

Once they had settled in one place, people started watching and keeping track of wild herds that could provide them with meat. Goats and sheep were the first animals to be farmed, initially for their meat alone. Pigs and cows were tamed a while later. People also started milking goats—long before cows. South American farmers kept llamas, turkeys, and guinea pigs.

Mud bricks and bitumen used for the construction of an ancient wall in Iraq

WALLS AROUND THE SETTLEMENT PROVIDED PROTECTION

Soon, settlements started taking shape. Homes became bigger, stronger and more permanent. Walls were built around the settlement to keep it safe. Once animals were domesticated, this became even more important because now they had to be protected from predators.

Sweet potatoes

WHAT WAS FARMED ELSEWHERE IN THE WORLD?

Later, as people settled in other parts of the world, they farmed crops that were native to those areas. Eight crops, including wheat, barley, lentils, and peas, were first grown in the Middle East. Farmers in South America grew maize and sweet potatoes.

BUILDING TOWNS AND CITIES

ONCE FOOD WAS PLENTIFUL, PEOPLE BEGAN TO EXPLORE

Jericho today

In some places, farmers were so successful that they started to produce more food than they could eat. People had time and resources to do other things—they could make pots or beads, or go out and trade. People began to exchange goods and services: villages grew bigger and more complex.

The ruins of Jericho, the oldest known city in the world

An ancient Ziggurat in ancient Sumer

CITIES DEVELOPED INTO BUSTLING URBAN CENTERS

The first cities were established about 5,000 years ago, built by the people of Sumer, also in the Middle East. They were constructed around huge temples called ziggurats, and had narrow winding streets packed with houses, shops, and inns. Each city could have been home to tens of thousands of citizens.

Çatalhöyük, Turkey

DOES JERICHO STILL EXIST?

Part of Jericho is still standing. There's a circular stone tower, with mud-plastered walls, where you can still see the plasterers' fingerprints.

The early towns housed many hundreds of people

The earliest town we know about is Jericho, in the Middle East. By about 8000 BCE, the town was surrounded by high stone walls and a deep ditch. Jericho was home to at least 2000 people. By 5000 BCE, around three times as many people were living in Çatalhöyük in Turkey, in a warren of mud-brick "boxes," with doors on the rooftops.

AMAZING!

It's thanks to the Sumerians' writing system that we have gotten to know so much about life in Sumer. The Sumerians were among the first to invent writing, and they wrote histories, love poems, hymns, shopping lists, and more. From their written records we learn the names of their rulers as well as the fact that both men and women wore skirts and makeup.

WILDLIFE

SPINELESS CREATURES

Coral reefs are a habitat for this brightly colored sponge.

MOST ANIMALS HAVE NO BACKBONE

As a matter of fact, about 90 percent of all the animals on Earth have no bones at all. They are called invertebrates and include 30 different groups of animals, ranging from the microscopic rotifer, to insects, and from big, wobbly jellyfish, to sponges. Invertebrates are cold-blooded, which means their body temperature is the same as the air or water around them.

The necklace sea star feeds on sponges and other invertebrates.

AMAZING!

Earthworms do not have a spine or any other bones. They have water-filled tubes, which run along the length of their bodies and act a little like a skeleton. Similarly, it is the pressure of body fluids that gives other invertebrates such as slugs and jellyfish their shape.

An earthworm burrows into the soil.

Many sea creatures are invertebrates

Sea stars, sea urchins, corals, sea anemones, as well as sponges, are all grouped as invertebrates. Some of these creatures, such as tubeworms, live at the bottom of the deepest ocean, where it is cold and totally dark.

The spiny lobster can grow as long as a man's forearm.

The fan tubeworm can withdraw its "fan" into a tube at its base.

MOST INVERTEBRATES GROW A HARD OUTER COVERING

This "outside skeleton," or exoskeleton, protects the soft, boneless body from injury and prevents it from drying up. In some groups of invertebrate, the exoskeleton is more obvious than in others: crustaceans, which include lobsters and crabs, develop an armor-like crust; mollusks such as snails, clams, and mussels grow shells—perfect places to hide.

Crabs live in water as well as on land.

HAVE YOU EVER WONDERED . . .

HOW DO CRABS GROW BIGGER INSIDE A SHELL?

A crab's hard shell cannot stretch. So, when a crab grows too big for its shell, it gets rid of it. The new shell underneath is already in place, and though it is soft at first, it soon hardens. A crab may need to change its shell as many as 20 times in its life!

CREEPY-CRAWLIES

Head Thorax Abdomen

Antenna Compound eye Wing

Ovipositor

Leg

Parts of an insect's body

ALL INSECTS HAVE A FEW THINGS IN COMMON

Although they may look different from one another, every adult insect has six legs and three parts to its body. The head is at the front, the thorax in the middle, and the abdomen at the back. Some may also have wings for flying, and long feelers or antennae.

Termite mounds can be taller than a tall basketball player.

MOST CREEPY-CRAWLIES PRODUCE LARGE NUMBERS OF EGGS

Insects form the food source for many reptiles, birds, and mammals. By laying a lot of eggs, insects make sure that at least some of them will make it to adulthood without getting eaten. For example, termite nests, which are air-conditioned mounds that can be up to 30 ft tall, are sometimes home to millions of termites and eggs.

Spiders are not insects

They have too many legs and too few body parts! A spider has eight legs, and its head and thorax are joined. Most also have eight eyes, though a few have six. More than 45,000 kinds of spiders are known to exist, but there are probably many more that have not yet been discovered. All spiders produce some venom, but very few are poisonous enough to cause much harm to humans.

Three kinds of insects on the same plant: a ladybird, some caterpillars and a butterfly.

The tarantula is one of the few spiders whose venom can cause serious harm to humans.

HAVE YOU EVER WONDERED...

HOW MANY INSECTS ARE THERE IN THE WORLD?

There are more insects in a square kilometre of forest than there are people on the entire planet! Creepy-crawlies live just about everywhere, under water, in caves, down deep holes and even on the tops of mountains. They make up 85 per cent of all known animal species, and there are probably millions more waiting to be discovered!

AMAZING!

An ants' nest is beautifully planned. It has many separate chambers, connected by a maze of tunnels. The rooms all have a specific function: some are nurseries for the eggs and the young; others are for storing food... they even have rubbish dumps!

The entrance to an ants' nest is surrounded by a mound of sand dug out to create the nest.

95

COLD-BLOODED AMPHIBIANS

The newt's moist skin helps it absorb oxygen.

AMPHIBIANS BREATHE THROUGH THEIR SKIN

Their thin, moist skin, which gives them the typical "slimy" look, allows oxygen to be absorbed into the blood from both the air and water. Amphibians start life in water and have gills so that they can breathe oxygen from the water. They also have fins, like fish. As they grow into adulthood, they develop lungs and can live on land, too.

Amphibians like being close to water.

HAVE YOU EVER WONDERED...

WHY SOME AMPHIBIANS ARE BRIGHTLY COLORED?

A number of amphibians are highly poisonous. This includes many types of frogs that sweat poison from the skin. Usually, the more brightly colored an amphibian is, the more toxic it is. The color warns predators to stay away.

Giant salamanders are the world's largest amphibians

They live in some rivers in China and can grow up to five feet in length, weighing in at over 110 pounds. They are eaten as a delicacy and are supposed to have medicinal properties, but are in danger of extinction in the wild.

Chinese giant salamander

They prefer to live not too far from water

Amphibians are cold-blooded, which means they cannot maintain their body temperature, but heat up or cool down depending on their surroundings. Damp soil and water bodies help them stay cool and moist. In addition, most amphibians lay soft, jelly-covered eggs in water, which is where the young are born and grow.

A red-eyed tree frog catches a meal.

ALL AMPHIBIANS ARE HUNTERS

Though they may eat plants when they are young, all adult amphibians are meat-eaters. They catch beetles, spiders, flies, worms, and even small fish for food. Many hunt at night, and have a sharp sense of hearing, smell, and eyesight. Some such as frogs flick out long, sticky tongues to catch prey.

Young frogs, called tadpoles, live only in water and breathe through gills, like fish.

Amphibians lay a clutch of soft, jelly-like eggs.

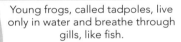

AMAZING!

The numbers of amphibians in the world have been declining steadily because of increasing pollution. A major reason for this is that amphibians absorb air and water through their skin, and so they are extremely sensitive and easily affected by pollution levels.

REPTILES: CROCODILES AND ALLIGATORS

Like amphibians, snakes, lizards, crocodiles, and turtles are also cold-blooded. They cannot maintain their body temperature and rely on the sun for heat. Although there are some species, such as sea snakes, that live in water, most reptiles do not need to live near water, as their hard, scaly skin prevents their bodies from drying out.

The fearsome "supercroc"

Crocodiles still look like dinosaurs

The relatives of today's reptiles were the dinosaurs, which ruled Earth for more than 200 million years. Though dinosaurs died out about 65 million years ago, there is a clear resemblance that is easy to see. In fact, today's crocodiles look very similar to *Sarcosuchus imperator*, a reptile from the prehistoric age, better known as "Supercroc."

American alligators eat everything from fruit to deer.

98

Tough crocodile skin

THEY COULD ALMOST BE ARMOR-PLATED

Both alligators and crocodiles are covered in tough, horny scales, strengthened with bone. When they are not lying almost submerged in water, waiting for a thirsty animal to come close enough that they can clamp their jaws on it, they can be found sunbathing on the banks.

AMAZING!

The biggest reptiles alive today are saltwater crocodiles. They're usually about 13 feet long, but a gigantic crocodile killed in 1957 measured twice as much—no less than 26 foot, and weighed almost 4,400 pounds!

Saltwater crocodiles can jump out of the water high into the air.

HAVE YOU EVER WONDERED...

HOW YOU CAN TELL A CROCODILE FROM AN ALLIGATOR?

You can tell them apart by their smile. While both the crocodile's and the alligator's top teeth will be visible when their mouths are shut, only the crocodile's bottom teeth will be poking out.

Not all crocodiles are big and scary

The dwarf caiman, which lives in South America, is the smallest crocodile. This mini croc grows only about five foot long—about a third of the size of its giant cousin, the massive saltwater crocodile.

The dwarf caiman has a dog-like head.

REPTILES: TORTOISES AND TURTLES

TORTOISES AND TURTLES ARE NOT THE SAME

While tortoises live on dry land and move around on short, stumpy legs, turtles prefer to live in water, and many of them have webbed feet to help them swim. Both have a beak-like mouth with no teeth. Sea turtles have flippers, because they live in the ocean and spend the majority of their lives under water. Most come to shore only to lay their eggs in nests buried in the sand.

HAVE YOU EVER WONDERED ...

DO ALL TURTLES HAVE HARD SHELLS?

There are some soft-shelled turtles that live in streams, rivers, lakes, and muddy ponds. They prefer not to lie around in the sun, and spend their time buried in mud or sand.

Softshell turtles lack scales on their shells.

A female leatherback crawls back into the ocean after laying eggs.

Tortoises are real slow pokes

Their heavy shells weigh them down so much that they move around very slowly, or not at all. Most tortoises lumber along at speeds of less than 0.27 miles per hour, even when they're hungry.

Turtles and tortoises have no teeth, as this hawksbill turtle's mouth reveals.

AMAZING!

The leatherback turtle is about the size of a small car. Weighing in at up to 2,000 pounds, this giant sea reptile can grow to lengths of almost 10 feet, from its head to the tip of its tail, and it has a similar flipper span. It can hold its breath for over 30 minutes to dive deep into the ocean.

THEY ARE THE LONGEST-LIVING ANIMALS ON LAND

Perhaps the secret to their long life is the tough, bony shell that protects them from dangerous predators. The oldest tortoise is believed to have been Adwaita, an Aldabra giant tortoise from the Seychelles, who lived in the Alipore Zoo in Kolkata (India). He was said to be about 250 years old when he died in 2006!

A 100-plus-year-old turtle from the Seychelles

A tortoise's shell reveals its age

Designed to protect the body, tortoise and turtle shells are made of bone and are covered in tough, horny plates. The reptiles' ribs and backbones are fused to the bones of the shells. Each year, the plates grow a new ring. If you count them, you can tell how old the tortoise is.

REPTILES: SLITHERING SNAKES

The Laotian wolf snake is active mostly at night.

A SNAKE'S BODY IS ENTIRELY COVERED WITH SCALES

Snakes are easily recognized by their long, thin, legless bodies. The scales that cover them can be smooth or rough, but are dry to touch. Special, transparent scales cover their eyes—snakes don't have eyelids, since they don't need to blink.

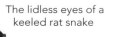

The lidless eyes of a keeled rat snake

The emerald tree boa can squeeze its prey to death.

HAVE YOU EVER WONDERED ...

WHY SNAKES SHED THEIR SKINS?

As a snake grows, its skin gets too small. So the snake grows a new skin underneath. Then, starting from the head and working down to the tail, it will slither out of the old one and leave it behind in one piece.

Shed snakeskin

Some snakes can hug you to death

Constrictors, like the anaconda or python, wrap their coils tightly around their prey. They don't crush their victims to death but squeeze them until they suffocate.

Though highly venomous to humans, the king cobra prefers eating other snakes.

AMAZING!

Since their sharp, backward-pointing teeth are good at holding food but not breaking it down, snakes have to swallow their prey whole. A snake has amazingly stretchy jaws. Elastic-like hinges join four separate jawbones, and there is no chin bone. This means their mouths open very wide to swallow food much larger than their heads, such as eggs and even deer!

A garter snake "sniffs" the air.

THEIR FANGS INJECT DEADLY VENOM

Most poisonous snakes are harmless to people. However, there are some such as cobras, rattlesnakes, and taipans whose poison is lethal to humans as well. Eight out of 10 of the world's deadliest snakes are found in Australia.

The inland taipan is one of Australia's deadliest snakes.

Snakes smell with their tongues

A snake's forked tongue constantly moves in and out of its mouth to pick up smells, in the form of tiny particles. These particles are then "tasted" through a very sensitive organ in the roof of the mouth.

REPTILES: SCURRYING LIZARDS

LIZARDS LOVE SUNBATHING

A green lizard enjoys the warmth of the sun.

Like all reptiles, lizards are cold-blooded. Cold lizards are sluggish and slow, so they warm up in the sun, before they can scurry off to hunt. The speediest lizard is the spiny-tailed iguana. It can run at almost 21 miles per hour, about the same speed as a champion sprinter!

Close-up of suction pads under the gecko's feet

Geckos have special suction pads on their feet

This enables them to cling on as they run up smooth walls and walk upside down across ceilings. They also have see-through eyelids. These are clear flaps of skin that protect their eyes from dust and dirt. Since the gecko can't blink to clean its eyelids, it sticks out its tongue and licks them clean!

AMAZING!

The basilisk lizard, which lives near rivers in South America, escapes from its enemies by running across water. It runs so fast on its long, fringed back toes that it doesn't have time to sink!

The poisonous Mexican beaded lizard

MOST LIZARDS ARE HARMLESS

Of the 3,800 different kinds of lizards, only two are poisonous: the Gila monster and the Mexican beaded lizard. Unlike snakes, these lizards do not have fangs, but bite their victims and chew poison into the wound instead.

HAVE YOU EVER WONDERED ...

WHAT DO CHAMELEONS KEEP STARING AT?

Chameleons can look two ways at once! They move each of their large, bulging eyes independently, so they can look in two different directions at once. When they're hunting, one eye can look out for tasty insects to eat. The other can watch out for hungry enemies.

The dinosaur-like Komodo dragon is found on a few islands in Indonesia.

Rinca, one of the islands that are home to the Komodo dragon.

Some are dragon-like and scary

The Komodo dragon, found on some islands in Indonesia, is the world's largest lizard. Males can grow to more than 10 foot in length and weigh more than 330 pounds. They are meat-eaters and can swallow pigs and deer whole!

The nearby water body offers a quick escape route to this basilisk.

FISH: A LIFE IN WATER

West African lungfish

FISH DIE WHEN TAKEN OUT OF WATER

Most fish cannot breathe air. They have slits, called gills, on the sides of their heads. Blood vessels in the gills absorb oxygen from the water that flows in, then release carbon dioxide into the water as it flows out, just like our lungs do from the air we breathe.

Freshwater carp

HAVE YOU EVER WONDERED ...

WHY DON'T FISH SINK?

Most fish have a swim bladder that has just the right amount of air to balance them in the water. It prevents them from either sinking or floating. Sharks do not have a swim bladder so they have to keep moving to avoid sinking.

These hammerhead sharks must keep swimming to avoid sinking.

Salmon swimming upstream jump against the flow of waterfalls

AMAZING!

The oldest, and the most primitive, bony fish are the lungfish. Although they have both gills and lungs and can survive out of the water by breathing air, most lungfish do need their bodies to remain moist. The West African lungfish is unique in that, when water levels drop, it burrows into the mud, spits out mucus to build itself a cocoon and goes to sleep until it rains—even if that takes two years!

FISH LIVE IN ALL TYPES OF WATER BODIES

There are over 30,000 species of fish. Lakes, ponds, streams, rivers, oceans… all are homes to fish. Fish of all shapes, sizes, and colors can be found in saltwater and fresh water, cold and warm temperatures, on the surface of seas and in the depths of the ocean.

The gills of a freshwater carp

They have a skeleton

In fact, fish were the first animals to develop a skeleton inside their bodies when they evolved 500 million years ago. They have a strong, flat tail, which pushes them through water, and fins, which help them change direction. However, only some fish are bony. Sharks and rays have skeletons of rubbery cartilage.

Haikouichthys was possibly the earliest-ever fish.

FISH: CURIOUS CREATURES

Manta ray

The dwarf goby is as long as a fingernail.

SOME FISH DON'T HAVE JAWS

Lampreys and hagfish have what can be called a sucker. Rows of small teeth circle the edge of the sucker, while longer ones are arranged around the edge of the mouth. Some of these fish are parasites, attaching themselves to other fish and living off the blood they suck; others feed on dead fish.

Suckers rim the mouth of the sea lamprey.

HAVE YOU EVER WONDERED ...

WHY DO SOME FISH SWIM IN GROUPS?

A group of fish is known as a school. For small fish, a school offers protection, because attacking fish may not be able to catch anything in the confusion. The tight formation may also fool predators because it resembles a large fish from afar.

AMAZING!

At a third of an inch long, the dwarf goby is the tiniest fish in the world. The whale shark is the biggest. It can reach lengths of about 40 feet from nose to tail, but is quite harmless to people. The biggest bony fish is the ocean sunfish, which can grow to over 10 foot in length, measuring more than 13 feet from top fin to bottom fin.

Manta rays "fly" through the water

Rays are flat-bodied fish with triangular, wing-like fins that make them look a little like birds. They are similar to sharks in that their skeletons are made of cartilage rather than bone. Unlike sharks, however, manta rays are harmless filter feeders, feeding on plankton and small fish, which they filter out of the water while moving.

Blue sea star on a coral reef

Starfish are not fish

Though commonly known as starfish, these marine animals are actually related to sea urchins and sand dollars. Scientists have renamed them with the more accurate label "sea stars."

SEAHORSES ARE ACTUALLY FISH

Seahorses get their name because their head resembles a horse's, but they have fins and a tail, and they breathe through gills, making them fish. The father seahorse takes care of the eggs before they hatch, by carrying them around in a pouch. When they hatch, hundreds of tiny seahorses squirt out.

Mediterranean seahorse

FISH: DEADLY SHARKS

A diver photographs a whale shark

SHARKS ARE MEAT-EATING SEA FISH

Most have sleek bodies and rows of sharp teeth. There are over 400 shark species of different shapes and sizes, living in different parts of the world. The dwarf shark is only four inches long, while the whale shark, the biggest of all fish, can reach lengths of 40 feet or more.

HAVE YOU EVER WONDERED . . .

ARE ALL SHARKS DANGEROUS?

In the order of dangerous sharks, the great white is most feared by people. Other dangerous sharks include the tiger shark, shortfin mako, and bronze and blacktip whalers, as well as the hammerhead. But most sharks are harmless to people and only attack if they are disturbed.

Sharks get very excited at the smell of blood

They can smell a drop of blood, diluted millions of times, almost half a mile away, and depend much more on their sense of smell than sight. In addition, a sensitive "lateral line" along their bodies allows them to feel ripples in the water created by an agitated animal or person, even when there is no blood to smell.

Sharks are ancient creatures

Fossils show that sharks appeared more than 350 million years ago, long before the dinosaurs. Megalodon was a huge shark that hunted large prey, and probably ate shellfish, too. The largest megalodon tooth found is almost seven inches long.

Sharks can swim in tight circles.

The shortfin mako shark is the fastest animal in the ocean.

Fossilised teeth of the megalodon

SHARKS ARE SPEEDY SWIMMERS

Their sleek shape means they can move quickly through the water and turn sharply, even at high speed. Sharks such as the shortfin mako are perfect swimming machines, capable of speeds up to 46 miles per hour.

AMAZING!

Many kinds of sharks would drown if they stopped swimming, since oxygen-rich water would no longer pass over their gills. They also swim all their lives to avoid sinking, because, unlike other fish, they do not have a swim bladder, though they do have a huge oily liver that helps keep them afloat.

The chain catshark is one of the most beautiful shark species.

BIRDS OF A FEATHER

Tropical birds often have colorful feathers—above are feathers of nine different bird species from Brazil.

ONLY BIRDS HAVE FEATHERS

There are around 9,000 different kinds of birds in the world. They are all warm-blooded, and all have two legs, two wings, and a beak. Most, but not all, can fly (though not all flying animals are birds). The one thing unique about birds is that all have feathers.

Different feathers have different purposes

Birds have three kinds of feathers. An inner layer of soft, downy feathers keeps them warm, and an outer, waxy layer keeps off the rain. Then there are the wing feathers that allow birds to fly.

A macaw displays its vibrant colors.

Some birds hide their colors; others flaunt them

The feathers that cover a bird's body are often so subtly colored that the bird is almost completely camouflaged; it can blend in with the surroundings and keep safe. Other birds, particularly the males of the species, make a statement and are more brightly colored to catch the female's attention.

A preening pair of jungle babblers

HOW MANY FEATHERS DO BIRDS HAVE?

Most birds have over 1,000 feathers, and some birds have many more. Swans have about 25,000 feathers—more than almost any other bird.

White swan

BIRDS DON'T LIKE RUFFLED FEATHERS

Birds frequently comb, or preen, their feathers with their beaks and claws, often preening each other. Most birds also spread oil on their feathers from a gland above the tail, to keep them waterproof.

AMAZING!

Some birds fly or migrate many thousands of miles each year, from feeding grounds to nesting grounds. The Arctic tern makes the longest migration flight. When summer ends in its Arctic nesting grounds, it flies to the Antarctic to catch the summer there, then flies back—a round trip of over 5,000 miles. In its lifetime, it flies a distance equal to three round trips to the Moon!

Arctic terns and kelp gulls in Antarctica

BIRDS ON THE WING

Horse | Lion | Human | Bird

Birds can support a lot of flesh and feathers on their thin, light wing bones.

BIRDS HAVE LIGHT, HOLLOW, BUT STRONG, BONES

The breastbone is usually quite large so that it can support the wing muscles. Birds flap their wings to take off and fly higher in the air. As the wing flaps down, the flight feathers close against the air, which pushes the bird up and forward. The tail balances the bird.

Owls are birds of prey with front-facing eyes.

BIRDS OF PREY CATCH AND EAT OTHER ANIMALS

They are excellent hunters, with strong, hooked beaks and sharp claws called talons, which are used to kill and tear prey. Their eyes are different from other birds' eyes—large, and front-facing—giving them superb vision and the ability to judge detail and distance.

Their wings are highly specialized

At almost 10 feet wide, the wandering albatross's wingspan is the largest of all flying birds. The huge wings allow the bird to glide almost effortlessly on air currents, and sometimes not land for weeks! Kestrels fly into the wind and beat their wings very quickly, hovering in the same position as they search for prey below. Tiny hummingbirds can hover and fly forward and sideways, as well as backward, flapping their wings at up to 90 beats per second.

The brilliantly colored garden emerald hummingbird

Wandering albatross

HAVE YOU EVER WONDERED . . .

WHY DO BIRDS SING?

Birds sing for many reasons. Most of all, they sing during the breeding season. A male bird sings to attract a mate, or to tell other birds to keep away from his territory. Males and females also call to warn other birds that an enemy such as a cat or a human is near.

The South American harpy eagle

AMAZING!

Eagles can catch animals much bigger and heavier than themselves.
The harpy eagle, which lives in South American jungles, is the biggest eagle of all. It has huge feet and scary talons, with which it grabs and crushes monkeys and other animals.

BIRDS: VARIED AND WONDROUS

BIRDS SIT ON THEIR EGGS TO KEEP THEM WARM

Most birds build nests to hide their eggs and to keep their young warm and safe from enemies. They don't leave their eggs alone for long, because if the eggs get cold the babies inside will die.

HAVE YOU EVER WONDERED . . .

WHY DON'T BIRDS FALL WHEN THEY SLEEP?

Birds have a long tendon attached to each toe. When they rest on branches or another perch, they bend their legs, and their toes lock around the perch.

A kittiwake gull guards its eggs

A blue waxbill curls its toes around a branch while it sleeps

Gentoo penguin

Not all birds need to fly

The wings of penguins serve as flippers in the water, where they turn into graceful swimmers. Ostriches, emus, rheas, kiwis, and other flightless birds run away from enemies. The African ostrich can sprint at over 37 miles per hour!

BIRDS HAVE DIFFERENT KINDS OF BEAKS BECAUSE THEY EAT DIFFERENT FOODS

The toucan uses its enormous beak to pull fruits from delicate branches. Parrots have short, curved, powerful beaks for cracking nuts and seeds, and, in some cases, for pulling themselves up trees. A woodpecker uses its unusual beak to drill for insects and to make nesting holes in dying trees. An eagle's hooked beak is perfect for tearing up meat. Herons have long beaks for spearing fish.

Biting into a pear is easy work for a toucan.

AMAZING!

The earliest bird-like creature that we know of lived 150 million years ago. *Archaeopteryx* had a head like a reptile, sharp teeth, a long tail, and feathered wings, used for gliding.

Hatchlings tap the egg with their beaks to crack it open

The young of tree-nesting birds are naked and blind when they hatch. They have to be fed by their parents till their flight feathers grow and they learn how to fly. On the other hand, the fluffy chicks of ground-nesting birds such as ducks can take care of themselves, and even go swimming, soon after they hatch.

Goose chicks start swimming with their mother soon after they are born.

MAMMALS: THE SMARTEST ANIMALS

Animals that are warm-blooded, have four limbs, breathe air, and have fur on their bodies are grouped as mammals. Most mammals give birth to live babies (though there are a few exceptions that lay eggs) and produce milk to feed their babies. Some spend their entire lives in water. Human beings are mammals, and hair is a type of fur—as are a porcupine's quills.

Springbok antelopes graze in the South African wilderness

They eat many kinds of food

Meat-eating mammals are called carnivores. Cats, dogs, lions, wolves, even insect-eaters such as hedgehogs come under this category. Mammals with hooves, such as goats, donkeys, cows, zebras, and antelopes, are all herbivores or plant-eaters. Mammals that eat both plants and other animals are omnivores.

A koala baby sits safely in its mother's pouch

WHICH IS THE TINIEST MAMMAL?

A flying mammal! The bumblebee bat that lives in caves in Thailand is only about one inch long, though its wingspan is about five inches.

Marsupials are also mammals

Koalas, wombats, possums, kangaroos, opossums, and Tasmanian devils are marsupials—a class of mammals that carry their young in pouches. For the first few months, the tiny baby lives inside the mother's pouch, feeding on milk. Even after it is old enough and jumping around on its own, a baby marsupial will dive into mommy's pouch at the first sign of danger.

Bottlenose dolphin

MAMMALS HAVE WELL-DEVELOPED BRAINS

They are often very intelligent. Of course, humans are the smartest, but there are other mammals that are quite smart, such as dolphins, pigs, dogs, and chimpanzees.

AMAZING!

Two types of mammals lay eggs: the platypus and the echidna. Platypus moms keep the eggs warm with their bodies until they hatch in about 10 days. They then feed the babies milk. Echidna moms keep their eggs safe in their pouches, where the babies hatch and drink milk.

Duck-billed platypus

MAMMALS IN WINTER AND WATER

SOME MAMMALS SLEEP THROUGH THE FREEZING WINTER

To conserve energy at a time when keeping warm would be difficult and finding food a big problem, many mammals hibernate or go into intermittent periods of deep sleep. As cold weather approaches, bears, dormice, and even some bats search for a safe comfortable place to curl up in. As they go into deeper sleep, their heartbeat and breathing slows down, and their body temperature drops. They live off their body fat, accumulated before winter. As soon as the days become warm, they wake up and get busy with living again.

American black bear

HAVE YOU EVER WONDERED . . .

WHICH ANIMAL SLEEPS THE LONGEST?

The American black bear is one of the world's champion snoozers. Its winter sleep lasts for seven months—over half of the year!

A humpback whale spouts through its blowholes

Whales breathe through blowholes

Whales have a hole at the top of their heads, like a flat nostril—some species have one; others two. This allows them to take in air without having to raise their heads above water. Muscles around the blowhole seal it tightly to prevent water from entering the whale's lungs when it is underwater. When whales blow out warm breath, it can shoot a misty spout in the cold air that can be as high as 40 feet!

NOT ALL MAMMALS LIVE ON LAND

Manatees, seals, dolphins, and whales live in water. Their front limbs have evolved into flippers and the back legs have fused into tails to help them swim better.

Seals can "walk" with their flippers.

A blue whale glides just under the surface of the ocean

AMAZING!

The blue whale is the largest animal in the world—so big that an adult human could crawl through its main blood vessel! A newborn baby blue whale is as big as a grown elephant, and can reach lengths of over 50 feet by the time it is six months old, feeding only on its mother's milk!

MAMMALS THAT EAT THEIR GREENS

HERBIVORE MAMMALS EAT ONLY PLANTS

Their front teeth are designed to grip and pull at plant matter, while the back ones are large and flat in order to grind it up. Herbivores tend to live in large groups, sometimes together with other mammals, for safety. Since they are preyed on by meat-eaters, they live in a constant state of high alert.

HAVE YOU EVER WONDERED . . .

HOW MUCH DOES AN ELEPHANT NEED TO EAT?

Most herbivores spend a large part of the day eating. Large animals like elephants need about 280 pounds of food a day to keep them going. That's a lot of vegetation to consume and could take up to 18 hours of grazing!

Elephants use their powerful trunks to rip off vegetation and pack it into their mouths.

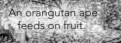
An orangutan ape feeds on fruit.

SOME ANIMALS OCCUPY THE TOPS OF TREES

Monkeys, apes, lemurs, bushbabies, and lorises are all primates. They are herbivores who find safety from predators high up in the trees. Their long, strong arms and legs, with fingers and toes that grip tightly, make them excellent climbers.

Some herbivores stand around chewing the cud

Deer, giraffe, and cattle are ruminants. While they graze, they simply chew a little and swallow the grass or leaves into a special part of the stomach, where it is softened. Later, while sitting or standing quietly, alert to predators, they bring up or regurgitate the cud—which is what the half-chewed food is called—and chew it properly.

Giraffes are the tallest mammals: their legs are just under six foot long—that's the same height as a tall human.

AMAZING!

Some herbivores are picky eaters who will eat only one particular part of one particular plant. Pandas eat only bamboo; koalas eat only leaves of the eucalyptus plant; and red tree voles eat only the needles of the Douglas fir tree. Others eat any plant matter available, from the bark of trees to roots, and even small branches.

MAMMALS THAT HUNT

Weasel

CATS, DOGS, AND BEARS ARE CARNIVORES

Many other mammals such as hyenas, weasels, raccoons, and also many humans, eat meat. Carnivores—except humans—usually have claws and long, sharp teeth that help them catch and tear their prey apart.

The cheetah is the fastest animal

It can reach speeds of close to 60 miles per hour—but only for a very short sprint. This cat normally runs down its prey within 820 feet and takes less than 20 seconds to catch its meal! But the speed king soon runs out of steam. If an impala keeps out of reach for more than 1,600 feet, it is safe—at least this time!

The Arctic fox in perfect camouflage

AMAZING!

Some mammals change their coats to match the season. Hares, foxes, and wolves in the snowy north fall into this group. Their brown coats turn white in winter for camouflage against the snow. The fur also grows extra thick to keep out the cold. These soft, white coats used to be highly prized, and the animals were hunted as a result.

Most canines live and hunt in packs

Jackals, for example, live in very close-knit family groups, sharing all the jobs. Sometimes a young female jackal may stay at home watching over the cubs, while all the other mothers go out hunting. Wolves and African wild dogs also hunt as a pack. First, they spread out, so they have a good view of the landscape, and then they close in on their prey. They keep in contact with each other through barks, howls, and body language.

Polar bear

A pack of wild dogs in Africa

The speedy cheetah

POLAR BEARS SWIM IN THE ICE-COLD ARCTIC

About 10 times heavier than a grown-up person, the powerful polar bear is the biggest of all meat-eating land mammals. These bears roam across northern Europe, northern Asia, and North America. If the Arctic Ocean isn't frozen, they swim, protected by thick fur and a layer of fat. Adult bears snack on fish and seals, and even beluga whales.

HAVE YOU EVER WONDERED . . .

WHY ARE ZEBRAS STRIPED?

In the heat haze of the African plains, the black and white stripes seem to wobble and confuse lions and other predators. Each zebra has its own pattern, so stripes might also help foals find their moms in the herd.

ABOUT
MYSELF

WHAT MAKES YOU, YOU

Sometimes two babies grow in the mother's womb at the same time.

THERE IS ONLY ONE PERSON LIKE YOU IN THE WHOLE WIDE WORLD

Even in a crowd of humans, those who know you would recognize you. Your skin is a particular color; your face is shaped in a certain way; your eyes and nose; how tall you are; the way you walk and talk; all these together make you unique, different from everyone else.

Every person on Earth is different.

HAVE YOU EVER WONDERED . . .

WHAT IS YOUR BELLY BUTTON?

Your belly button is where you were once joined to your mother. A baby grows inside its mother's womb for nine months. It gets all the food and oxygen it needs to grow through a long tube called the umbilical cord. When the baby is born, this cord is cut. What remains is the belly button, or the navel.

A doctor cuts and clamps a newborn baby's umbilical cord.

AMAZING!

Identical twins develop from one fertilized egg that splits into two. The two babies will be the same sex and very similar in appearance. Whereas non-identical twins are formed when two separate eggs are fertilized. The babies may be the same sex or different and will be no more alike in appearance than other siblings.

YOU INHERIT YOUR GENES FROM YOUR PARENTS

Genes are carried in your father's sperm and your mother's egg. Genes determine the characteristics that are passed on to you from your parents.

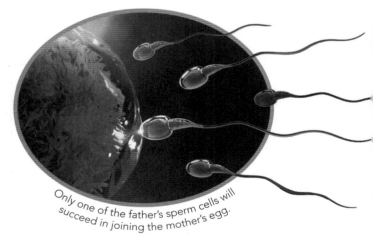

Only one of the father's sperm cells will succeed in joining the mother's egg.

You started off as one tiny cell

You began when a sperm from your father joined with an egg from your mother. A cell, no bigger than the tip of a pin, formed and began to divide into more and more cells, until they formed a baby. That baby was YOU.

YOUR AMAZING BODY

ABOUT 50 BILLION TINY CELLS MAKE UP YOUR BODY

Different kinds of cells have different functions. These cells get instructions on how to grow and work from genes—half of which come from your mother, and half from your father.

When your body functions well, you are healthy.

GROWING UP TAKES TIME

You will get taller and stronger, and continue changing shape, until you're about 18 to 21 years old. After that you will stop growing, though your muscles continue to develop in response to how much you work them.

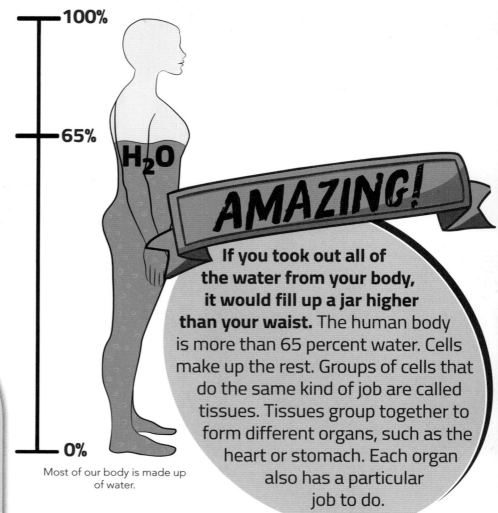

100%

65%

H₂O

0%

Most of our body is made up of water.

AMAZING!

If you took out all of the water from your body, it would fill up a jar higher than your waist. The human body is more than 65 percent water. Cells make up the rest. Groups of cells that do the same kind of job are called tissues. Tissues group together to form different organs, such as the heart or stomach. Each organ also has a particular job to do.

Your body works as a whole

The parts of your body—both the outside parts, like your arms and legs, and the inside parts, like your heart, bones, and muscles that you can't see at all, work together like the different parts of a machine, so you can laugh, cry, walk, jump, read, and sleep . . .

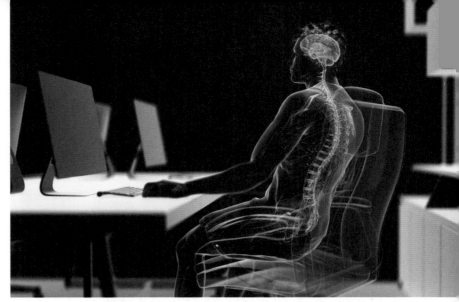

Even while sitting, different parts of your body—brain, muscles, bones, heart, lungs—are all working together.

Every tissue has its own group of cells

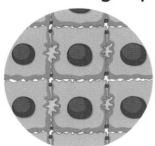

Intestinal cells

Blood cells

Liver cells

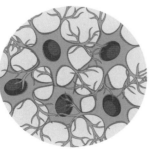

Nerve cells

Stem cells

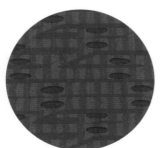

Muscle cells

HAVE YOU EVER WONDERED . . .

WHY DO YOU GET SICK AT TIMES?

You get sick when tiny, harmful germs get into your body. They interfere with your cells and prevent them from doing their jobs. Special protector cells, called white blood cells, have to rush in to destroy the germs by eating them up to make you better again. Sometimes, if the germs are too strong, your white blood cells need a little help from the doctor.

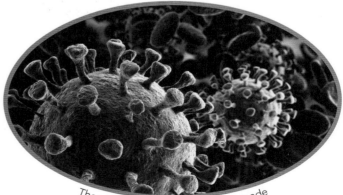

These are coronavirus germs that made millions of people sick across the world.

THE ARMOR YOUR BODY WEARS

YOUR SKIN IS THE FIRST LINE OF PROTECTION FOR YOUR BODY

As you grow, your skin grows with you. It fits you like a glove, keeping out dirt and germs that could cause infection, and preventing you from becoming too cold or too hot. In addition, your skin contains oil that helps to make it waterproof. If cut or hurt, it heals itself and new skin grows over the injured area.

The thickest skin is on the underside of the feet.

Skin creates scar tissue to heal itself.

AMAZING!

The thickness of your skin varies across different parts of your body. It's thickest on the palms of the hands and soles of the feet, and thinnest on your eyelids. The cells of the top layer of your skin are constantly being replaced. In fact, a lot of the dust around your home is actually skin, since the human body sheds approximately 40,000 flakes of skin every minute!

Hair is the human version of fur

It keeps the head from getting too hot or too cold and also protects it from the Sun's harmful ultraviolet rays. Hair grows out of tiny holes in our skin. If the hole is round, then hair grows straight; curly hair grows out of oval-shaped holes. Only the palms and soles of your hands and feet don't have any hair.

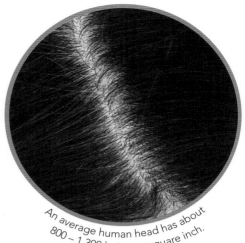

An average human head has about 800 – 1,300 hairs per square inch.

NAILS ARE VERY IMPORTANT

Made of keratin, the same stuff that makes up skin and hair, the nails protect the tips of your fingers and toes, and very often indicate how healthy you are. Smooth, clean nails of a nice, pink color tell the doctor that you are doing well.

Healthy nails

Melanin is what causes freckles.

HAVE YOU EVER WONDERED...

WHY ARE SOME PEOPLE FAIR AND OTHERS DARK?

Skin contains a special coloring called melanin. This protects it from the Sun's harmful rays, which can burn the skin. Dark skin has more melanin than pale skin.

YOUR BONY FRAMEWORK

BONES GIVE THE BODY ITS SHAPE

If you did not have bones, you'd be like a shapeless, floppy jellyfish, unable to stand. It is your bones that help you make lots of different movements. They also help to protect the soft parts inside your body: the skull protects your brain, and the ribs protect your heart and lungs.

BONES ARE HARD AND STRONG

Inside the hard outer layer is another layer of soft, spongy bone. Most of the bones in the body are made of a mineral called calcium, and some are full of mushy stuff called marrow. Some of this marrow makes new red and white blood cells.

Marrow

AMAZING!

You had about 300 bones when you were born. As you grow, some bones fuse to become a single bone, so an adult has fewer bones. Your bones will continue to grow till you are about 25 years old, so you will get taller and heavier. More than half the bones in your body are in your hands and feet!

Joints allow the bones to move

The bones in your body join up to make a frame called the skeleton. Joints are where the bones come together. Some joints are immovable, but others allow the bones to be moved in different directions. The edges of the bones at these joints are protected by something called cartilage, which makes it possible for them to rub against each other smoothly and not get worn down.

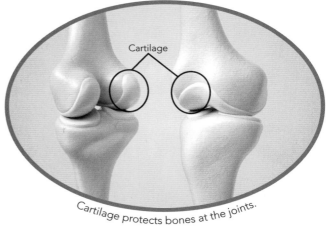

Cartilage protects bones at the joints.

The human skeleton

WHICH IS THE SMALLEST BONE IN YOUR BODY?

The smallest is a tiny bone that is located in the middle portion of your ear. It is called the stapes, or the stirrup bone, and it is less than three millimeters long. Its job is to carry sound vibrations to the inner ear. The longest bone is the femur, which is your thigh bone.

The stirrup bone in the ear looks like the stirrup used for horse riding.

Stirrup bone

Eardrum

MUSCLE POWER

MUSCLES CONTROL ALL MOVEMENT IN YOUR BODY

You have more than 600 muscles to help you move different parts of your body. Muscles in your arms lift and pull. Muscles in your thumbs enable you to hold things. Muscles in your chest help you to breathe. Your heart muscles keep it beating. Almost half the weight of your body is muscle weight.

Skating is difficult at first but becomes easier as you practice.

AMAZING!

If you do something over and over again, your muscles will "learn" how to do it, getting more precise and accurate over time. The action becomes part of your "muscle memory" and allows you to react instinctively. This is why it is said, "practice makes perfect."

Stomach muscles work on their own.

SOME MUSCLES WORK ON THEIR OWN

There are some muscles that wait for you to tell them what to do—kick a ball, or take a spoon to your mouth. Other muscles, such as those that push food down your throat when you swallow, or the muscles of your heart, are not controlled by you—they know what they have to do.

Exercise is good for the muscles

Exercise works the muscles and makes them stronger and bigger. It also keeps them flexible. Not using muscles causes them to shrink and become weak.

Push-ups strengthen the chest and arm muscles.

Tightening and relaxing muscles moves your bones

Muscles are attached to your bones across joints, and usually work in pairs. When one muscle contracts, the other relaxes, pulling the bone one way. When the first one relaxes and the second contracts, the bone moves back again.

Curling up a dumbbell contracts the muscles in the front of the arm while the ones behind relax.

HAVE YOU EVER WONDERED...

WHICH MUSCLE IS THE MOST HARD-WORKING?

The cardiac muscle of your heart does the most work: it is on the job each and every moment of your life.

137

WHAT HAPPENS WHEN WE EAT

FOOD HAS TO BE DIGESTED

The food that you eat has vitamins and minerals needed by your body for energy—to grow, stay healthy, and do things. But all the nutritious elements in food are locked within complex substances. Before your body can absorb the nutrients, the substances must be broken down through a process called digestion.

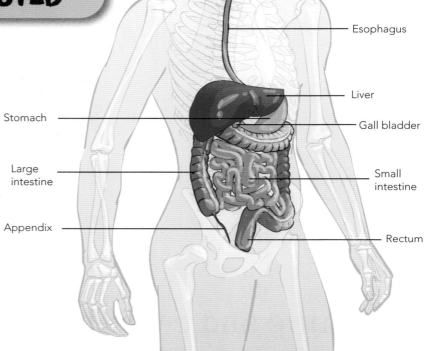

Mouth

Esophagus

Liver

Stomach

Gall bladder

Large intestine

Small intestine

Appendix

Rectum

You have two intestines

The small intestine is about 23 feet long. The first part continues to break down food, while the second absorbs nutrients into the blood. Whatever cannot be used is sent on to the five foot long large intestine, to be passed as waste.

AMAZING!

The juices produced by your stomach are acidic. They help kill bacteria that you may have eaten with the food. The stomach has a very, very thick lining to prevent this acid from harming you.

Digestion is a long process

In your mouth, the teeth crush the food and mix saliva into it before pushing it down a long tube going from your mouth into your stomach. Juices in your stomach mush the food into a soup before squeezing it through long, coiled tubes called intestines. There, whatever the body needs is absorbed from the food, and the rest is pushed out as waste.

Chewing is only the beginning of the digestive process.

Good bacteria (in green) in the intestines help control digestion.

HAVE YOU EVER WONDERED . . .

WHY DOES YOUR STOMACH RUMBLE SOMETIMES?

The walls of your stomach and intestines rumble as they contract and expand. You can hear them more when your stomach is empty because food muffles the sound.

FOOD STAYS IN THE STOMACH FOR HOURS

Juices, called enzymes, produced by the lining of the stomach, need time to slowly break up your food and release the goodness. It takes about four hours before what you have eaten is ready to go to the small intestine.

If you eat too much your stomach may feel very full.

YOUR LIFEBLOOD

BLOOD KEEPS EVERY TINY PART OF US ALIVE

Blood carries oxygen and goodness from the food you eat to all the tiny cells in your body to keep them alive and working properly. It also picks up the waste they generate and takes it away so the body can get rid of it. While doing all this, it also spreads heat so that your fingers and toes remain as warm as the rest of you.

A 3-D illustration of the male arterial system

You are alive and active because of the blood circulating in the body.

AMAZING!

It takes approximately 62,000 miles of blood vessels to provide each and every cell of your body with the oxygen and energy it needs to stay healthy! An adult's heart beats about 70 times a minute, pushing out a cupful of blood with every beat, to keep this network working.

Blood circulates around the body

It travels around your body in narrow tubes called blood vessels. Arteries carry blood rich with oxygen and nutrients to every part of your body. Smaller capillaries pass this on to the cells, take oxygen–poor blood back and connect with veins. Veins carry the oxygen-poor blood back to your heart, which replenishes it and pumps it out to the arteries again.

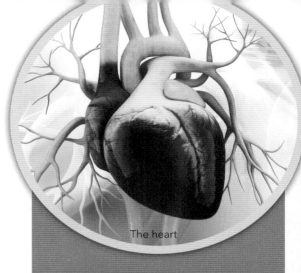

The heart

THE HEART IS THE CONTROL CENTER

Your heart is a special muscle that keeps working all the time, even when you're fast asleep. It is located in the middle of your chest, a little bit to the left, between your lungs. About as big as your fist, your heart is strong enough to pump blood all around your body whether you are standing, jumping, running, or lying down.

HAVE YOU EVER WONDERED . . .

CAN I FEEL MY HEART BEATING?

If you've been running, you can sometimes feel your heart beating in your chest. Running makes your heart beat faster so more blood gets to the muscles that are doing the extra work—in this case, the legs. Normally, if you put your fingers on the inside of your wrist, you can feel the steady throb of your blood moving in time to your heartbeat.

You can feel your pulse inside the wrist.

A BREATH OF FRESH AIR

LIVING THINGS NEED OXYGEN TO STAY ALIVE

If their oxygen supply was cut off, the cells in the body would quickly die—within seconds. This essential oxygen is supplied to cells in every part of your body by what is called the respiratory system. At the center of this system are your lungs.

Nostril

Larynx

Right lung

Diaphragm

The vocal cords are located in the larynx.

AMAZING!

The respiratory system helps you speak. When you want to speak, sing, or make a noise, you breathe in and force air out through your vocal cords in your throat. This makes them vibrate and creates different sounds. This is why you cannot speak when you are out of breath!

Breathing moves air in and out of the lungs

In the lungs, oxygen from the air you breathe in is absorbed into the bloodstream to be carried to the rest of your body by the pumping heart. At the same time, the waste carbon dioxide, carried by the blood from your cells into the lungs, is released into the air you breathe out. If this carbon dioxide remained in your blood, it would poison you.

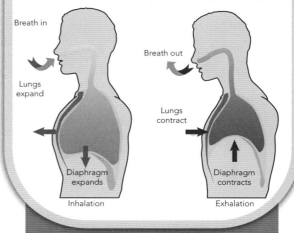

The movements of the chest during breathing

Breath in
Lungs expand
Diaphragm expands
Inhalation

Breath out
Lungs contract
Diaphragm contracts
Exhalation

Trachea

Left lung

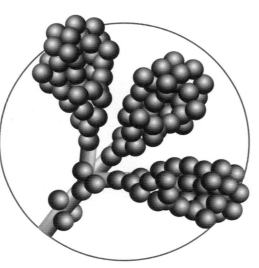

The exchange of oxygen and carbon dioxide in the lungs takes place in small sacs called alveoli.

THE DIAPHRAGM HELPS YOU BREATHE

This is a muscle that lies just below your lungs. When you breathe out, your chest and lungs become smaller, and the diaphragm arches upward to squeeze out stale air. As you breathe in, the diaphragm flattens, your chest expands, and your lungs get bigger; air rushes up your nose, down your windpipe, and into your lungs. All this happens in just a few seconds.

HAVE YOU EVER WONDERED . . .

WHY DO I YAWN?

It happens when you haven't been breathing deeply, because you're tired, or have been sitting still for a long time and have not been getting enough oxygen. To take in more oxygen, your body makes you take a big gulp of air through the mouth.

You often yawn when you wake up because it helps the body to stretch out the lungs.

BOSS OF THE BODY

YOUR BRAIN TELLS YOU WHAT TO DO

Your brain controls how you think, feel, and behave. It stores all that you have learned, all your emotions, your thoughts and memories, worries, and dreams. Based on all this information, it tells your body how to work, and controls everything you do. The brain is really very smart.

Thirty-one pairs of nerves branch out from the spinal cord to the whole body.

The spinal cord can also control reactions

Sometimes the body reacts automatically, even before the message has reached the brain. This is a reflex action, which is controlled by the spinal cord. An example of this is when your throat or a nostril gets irritated and you cough or sneeze without thinking.

AMAZING!

The brain has two clear halves. When the nerves enter the brain, they cross. As a result, the left side of the brain controls the right side of the body, while the right half controls the left side of the body. And, though it does not move, the brain works hard enough to use about 20 percent of the body's energy.

Nerves are the brain's messengers

They carry messages, in the form of tiny electric pulses, to and from your brain. Nerves run from your spinal cord—a thick rope of nerves inside your backbone—to every part of your body. Together with the brain, they make up your nervous system.

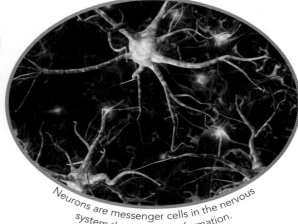

Neurons are messenger cells in the nervous system that transmit information.

The brain

IS A BIG BRAIN SMARTER THAN A SMALLER ONE?

The human brain is about three times bigger than that in other mammals of the same size, and humans are definitely the smartest animals. Among humans, however, having a brain bigger in size does not mean that the person is smarter.

YOUR SENSES INFORM THE BRAIN WHAT'S UP

Your five senses—sight, hearing, touch, smell, and taste—are constantly in touch with your brain, letting it know what is happening all around, so that it can tell the body how to react.

The brain decides whether what you sense is good or bad.

SEEING AND HEARING

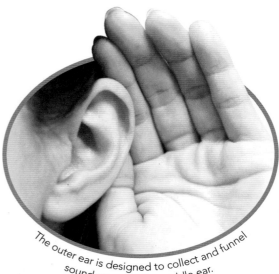

The outer ear is designed to collect and funnel sound waves to the middle ear.

THE EYES SEND PICTURES TO THE BRAIN

Each of your eyes is a ball. Inside the ball, at the front, there's a black hole called the pupil, which lets in light. This light lands on the retina at the back of the eye as an upside-down image. The retina converts these images into electric signals and sends them to the brain through the optic nerve.

Visual cortex

Eye

Optic nerve

Superior rectus muscle

Lens

Sclera

Cornea

Pupil

Ciliary body

Retina

Fovea

Optic disc

Optic nerve

Diagram of an eye
The visual cortex of the brain is where the image is decoded.

Ears catch sound waves

The flappy, outer parts of your ears collect sounds from the air, which enter your ears as tiny, invisible waves. These waves make your eardrum move up and down, which makes tiny bones deep inside your ears vibrate as well. This vibration is carried to the liquid in the inner ear, where it is converted into electric signals for the brain.

In the dark   In a brightly lit place

The size of the pupil varies according to the available light.

HAVE YOU EVER WONDERED . . .

WHY DO YOU HAVE TWO EYES AND TWO EARS?

Two eyes send the brain the same pictures from slightly different angles. The brain compares the two and is able to accurately calculate how far or how near things are. With two ears on either side of the head, it is easier to figure out the direction of a sound.

THE EYES CONSTANTLY ADJUST TO LIGHT

The muscles in and around the eye automatically try and make sure you see as clearly as possible. For example, the pupils become smaller when it is very bright, so that less light enters each eye. At night, or when it is dark, the pupils open wide to catch every bit of light, so that you can see.

AMAZING!

The fluid in your inner ear also helps you balance. The brain compares how this fluid is moving, and the angle at which it is tilted, with information it receives from the eyes. When you spin fast for a while and then stop, the dizziness you experience is because your brain is confused: your eyes tell it that you are not moving but the fluid in the inner ear is still spinning!

The ears not only hear but also help you balance.

SMELLING AND TASTING

YOU SMELL WITH THE TINY HAIRS IN YOUR NOSE

Your nose is divided into two nostrils. When you breathe in, the air that enters your nostrils passes over small cells at the top of the nasal passage. These cells are covered with tiny hairs that trap the smell and send nerve signals up to the brain to be decoded.

The nostrils

YOUR SENSE OF SMELL AND TASTE WORK TOGETHER

If you're eating a freshly baked cookie, your nose smells how sweet it is and the taste buds on your tongue pick up its flavor. The brain combines the two and tells you that the cookie is delicious!

If your nose is congested, you cannot taste properly.

The nose can detect the difference in smell between a peach and an apricot.

Your tongue has tiny taste buds

These are called papillae, and there are about 10,000 of them on your tongue. Each is covered with lots of tiny hairs. When saliva mixes with food, it dissolves the flavors and carries them across the tongue. The hairs detect them and send off signals to the brain to decipher.

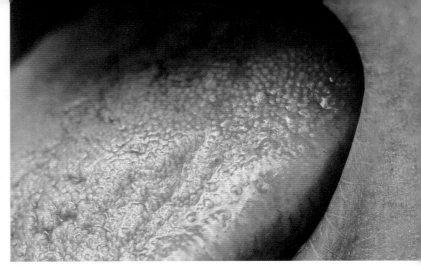

You can see the taste buds on the surface of the tongue.

Different taste buds taste different flavors

The tongue can taste four different flavors: sweet, sour, salty, and bitter. At one time, scientists thought that taste buds for each were located on particular parts of the tongue, but now they think that, perhaps, they are mixed up.

HAVE YOU EVER WONDERED . . .

WHY DOES FOOD TASTE FUNNY WHEN YOu HAVE A COLD?

If your nose is congested, the brain gets only half the information on whatever you eat, so it processes it differently, making even familiar food taste weird.

AMAZING!

Your nose can pick up over 10,000 smells!
Smells that float in the air are actually tiny particles that are not visible. Sometimes, when you don't recognize a smell, you might sniff. This draws more particles into the nose to help you figure out the smell.

THE SCIENCE BEHIND STUFF

SOLIDS, LIQUIDS, AND GASES

EVERYTHING AROUND US TAKES ONE OF THREE FORMS

A solid has a particular shape that does not change easily. A liquid flows and has to be held in a container, otherwise it will form a puddle. A gas can float away if it is not in a sealed container.

HAVE YOU EVER WONDERED . . .

WHAT IS STEAM?

When water is boiled and changes into water vapor, it floats up as an invisible gas. But when the vapor touches the cool air around it, it cools and starts to change back from an invisible gas into a liquid. At this stage, it can be seen because it is made up of lots of tiny droplets of liquid water. This is steam.

Steam rises from a hot water pool in America's Yellowstone National Park.

Forms keep changing

Most materials will change from a liquid into a gas if they are heated enough, and from a liquid into a solid, if they get cold enough. When water is heated, it changes into an invisible gas—water vapor—and floats away in the air. Ice is what forms when water gets very, very cold and freezes into a solid.

When you stir salt in water it "disappears."

DISAPPEARING ACT

If you add a spoonful of sugar or salt to a glass of water, it seems to vanish. However, you can tell it is there if you taste the water. It has not vanished but melted, or dissolved, into the water and become part of it.

Freezing winter temperatures turn the water of a lake into ice.

AMAZING!

The bubbles in soft drinks are the gas carbon dioxide. You can't see them when the top is on the bottle because the gas is dissolved in the liquid. But there is a lot of carbon dioxide that is squashed into the drink, and when you open the bottle the gas escapes as bubbles.

Carbon dioxide creates the froth and fizz as you pour out a soda.

WHAT PULLS YOU DOWN

THERE'S NO DENYING GRAVITY

Earth has an invisible force called gravity that pulls everything toward it, and stops things like soccer balls from flying off into space. This is why you fall "down," and when you jump "up" you have to make a real effort to get as high as you can before you fall back again.

If there was no gravity, we would all be floating around who knows where— that is, if we existed at all. It is the Sun's gravity that keeps Earth in its orbit, and Earth's gravity that keeps the atmosphere wrapped around it like a safety blanket. All the planets and stars have their own place in the Universe because of the way each object's gravity pulls or pushes at the others.

When you trip or lose your balance, you fall down because gravity pulls you to the ground.

Size and distance matter

The Moon has about one-sixth of Earth's gravity. The amount of gravity depends on the size of the object; larger objects have more gravity. Of course, how much this gravity can pull you toward it depends on how close you are to it.

Though both Earth and the Moon have gravity, between them there is no gravity and everything free-floats.

Skydivers jump, secure in the knowledge that gravity will pull them down to Earth.

DIVERS CAN CONTROL THEIR DESCENT

When skydivers jump out of an airplane, they drop toward the ground at about 118 miles per hour. They would fall faster, but the force of air pushing upward against the fall slows them down a bit. Opening a parachute increases air resistance and slows the skydiver down to about 12 miles per hour— though that feels fast enough when you're falling through the air!

HAVE YOU EVER WONDERED . . .

DOES GRAVITY PULL EVERYTHING WITH THE SAME FORCE?

Yes, it does. If there was no air, a dropped feather or stone would fall to the ground at the same time. Things fall at different speeds because of how air pushes upward against them and slows them down.

A MATTER OF WEIGHT

MASS DETERMINES WEIGHT

Weight is the effect of gravity on an object's mass, which is the amount of stuff or matter that it's made of. The more mass something has, the more gravity pulls it down, and the heavier it is. The reason why objects of the same size do not always weigh the same is because they don't have the same mass.

It will take many more balloons than these to equal the weight of the ice-cream tub.

AMAZING!

Like everything else on Earth, air has weight. It would take as many as 4,000 balloons to equal the weight of a tub of ice cream!

VOLUME IS THE SPACE AN OBJECT OCCUPIES

When you blow air into a balloon, it gets bigger; the air needs space, so it stretches the rubber balloon. The space it occupies is the volume of air inside the balloon. All things have volume, whether it is an invisible particle of gas or a mountain.

The space occupied by air is equal to its volume.

Mass varies

Mass depends on how tightly packed the matter inside an object is. Think of two jars—one full of sand and the other full of cotton. The jar of sand would be much heavier because the grains of sand fit tightly inside it and against each other, so there are more of them, and there is more mass. In comparison, the particles of cotton are much more loosely packed, with lots more empty spaces in between. It would take a lot more cotton to equal the weight of the jar of sand.

The object with denser mass is heavier.

WHY DOES WATER RISE WHEN YOU GET IN THE BATH?

It happens because your body pushes the water out of the way to make a space for you. And the only place the water can go is up, so its level rises. The amount the water rises is equal to the amount of space you are occupying in the water.

FLOATING ON AIR AND WATER

FLOATING BALLOONS ARE LIGHTER THAN AIR

Things float upward when they're lighter than the air around them. Air-filled balloons are roughly the same weight as the surrounding air, and drop to the ground. Balloons that really float up and fly away are filled with helium, a gas that's much lighter than air. It's used in airships, as well as in party balloons.

Lighter-than-air helium gas allows airships to fly.

The wings of an aircraft are designed to lift it into the air.

When this empty freighter ship is laden with cargo, it can sink up to the top of the red part of its hull.

The wings of an airplane are designed so that, when the plane moves forward, the airstreams passing over the upper and lower surfaces of the wings create lower pressure on top and higher pressure on the bottom. This difference in pressure creates an upward thrust, which lifts the plane. The engines of the plane keep it moving fast enough to keep this pressure steady and the plane flying.

Fish swim with an air bag.

FISH FLOAT WITH THE HELP OF AN AIR CHAMBER

Most fish have a gas-filled bag called a swim bladder inside them, which helps with buoyancy. By controlling the amount of air in this bag, the fish changes the depth at which it swims. When it wants to rise to the surface, the fish fills this bladder with oxygen it breathes in through its gills. When the bladder is empty, the fish can sink to the bottom.

HAVE YOU EVER WONDERED . . .

HOW DO BIG, HEAVY SHIPS MANAGE TO STAY AFLOAT?

Because their hulls are filled with air. The ship sinks in water to the point that the weight of the water it pushes aside matches its own weight and the weight of the air in it. How low the ship sits in water depends on how heavily laden it is, and how dense the water is.

Water pushes upward to help things float

When something is put in water, it pushes against an upward force called buoyancy created by the water. It can float only if it is lighter than the amount of water it pushes aside. If the object is heavier, the water's upthrust will not be strong enough to hold it up. Salty water has more upthrust than fresh water, and is easier to float in.

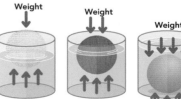

While cork has enough buoyancy to float easily, iron has none.

SEEING THE LIGHT

Sunbeams streak through a forest canopy

LIGHT IS A FORM OF ENERGY

The biggest source of light is the Sun, but there are also other sources that give out light, such as the tiny firefly and deep-sea creatures. Light is a form of energy that we can see. It travels from one place to another as a stream of tiny particles called photons.

HAVE YOU EVER WONDERED . . .

HOW LONG DOES IT TAKE LIGHT TO REACH US FROM THE SUN?

Scientists have measured how fast light travels, and . . . well, it's fast: 983,571,056 foot per second, to be exact. At that speed, it takes eight minutes for light from the Sun to reach Earth, and just 1.3 seconds for it to travel from the Moon to Earth!

Photon particles carry light from the Sun to Earth in less time than it takes you to eat your breakfast.

Ocean creatures called tunicates produce their own light.

Light bounces off surfaces

Trees, houses, and people don't give off their own light, even in the daytime. We can only see them because sunlight is bouncing off them into our eyes. This bouncing off is called reflection. Moonlight is sunshine reflecting off the Moon toward us.

Light reflecting off the girl's sunglasses forms the image of what she's looking at.

LIGHT TRAVELS IN STRAIGHT LINES

When light hits something flat and smooth like a mirror, it comes straight back—like a ball bouncing off a wall. You see yourself in a mirror because light bounces off your face toward the mirror, and then straight back into your eyes. If you look into rippling water, light bounces back at different angles, and the image your brain sees are ripples as well.

The rippling image is due to the way the light bounces off the water's surface.

AMAZING!

Some animals make their own light. They have special organs inside their bodies where light-producing chemicals react with oxygen breathed by the animal to create a glow. Many of these creatures, such as some kinds of jellyfish and tunicates, live in the deep sea, where it is always dark, and they use this glow to attract prey.

THE PLAY OF LIGHT

Doors block out light.

LIGHT CAN PASS THROUGH CERTAIN MATERIALS

When materials let light through, we call them transparent. Objects that reflect all the light, not letting any pass through, are called opaque. Thick curtains and wooden shutters can block light and make rooms dark, even during the day.

AMAZING!

Prisms have a special shape, so that light bends when it enters. What is really amazing is that some colors bend more, and others less. As a result, white light is split into its different colors. A clear, transparent prism shows a bright, sharp spectrum of colors; if it is translucent, the scattered light particles will make it fuzzy.

A prism breaks up the colors of light.

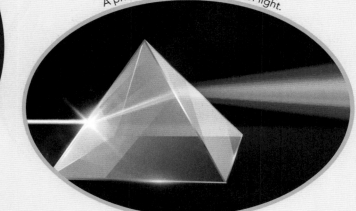

Light scatters

Some materials such as frosted glass, ice, and plastic are translucent—they allow light to pass through—but you cannot see clearly through them. This is because, when the rays of light pass through, the particles of light scatter, blurring the image.

A long shadow means it is early morning or late evening.

The frosted glass panes on both sides of the entrance to this office blur the light

YOUR SHADOW CAN TELL YOU THE TIME

Your body isn't transparent, so it blocks the light and makes a dark patch, which we call a shadow. If you stand with your back to the Sun, you can judge what time of the day it is by the length of your shadow. It is longest in the morning and evening. At 12 noon, when the sun is high in the sky, your shadow looks like a puddle around your feet.

HAVE YOU EVER WONDERED . . .

HOW DID PEOPLE TELL THE TIME BEFORE WATCHES WERE INVENTED?

The earliest device for telling time was a simple gnomon. It was used at least 5,500 years ago. All it consisted of was a pillar and some markings on the ground around it for different times of the day. As the day went by, the shadow created by the rod shifted over the markers, indicating the time. Imagine the shadow like a needle of a watch turning over the dial and pointing at the numbers. The gnomon is so simple that you can even make one at home!

Gnomon

Using sunlight, a sundial can tell the time. The gnomon casts a shadow that points to the time of day.

A WORLD IN COLOR

LIGHT IS LIKE THE RAINBOW

Sunlight is really a mixture of red, orange, yellow, green, blue, indigo, and violet. All these colors combine to make a brilliant white. White light is brightest because it contains all the light in a stream, or ray, of light.

THE SKY IS FILLED WITH SCATTERED BLUE LIGHT

The air around us has no color. The sky appears blue because the gases and dust in the air scatter light as it enters the atmosphere. The color blue gets scattered the most, and that is what we see.

It is the way light scatters that colors the sky.

A rainbow forms when light passes through raindrops

Sometimes, when it rains, the drops of water in the air break up the white light and spread it into all its colors. When this happens, we see a rainbow.

When water in the air breaks up rays of sunlight, a rainbow is formed.

Colors bounce back at us

When light hits something, only some of its colors are reflected. That is the mix of colors we see. Grass looks green because only green light bounces off it—the other colors of light are swallowed up. An object is white because it has reflected all the colors; on the other hand, something that is black has absorbed all of them.

Leopards can't see colors well.

AMAZING!

Generally speaking, animals that roam and hunt after dark have poor color vision. Dogs, cats, rabbits, and mice, for example, see colors as paler hues with a gray tint to them. Monkeys, birds, and squirrels can see colors almost as well as you can. Bees and butterflies have super vision, however, and can see the ultraviolet range of colors!

HAVE YOU EVER WONDERED...

Ozone layer

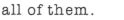

WHAT IS ULTRAVIOLET LIGHT?

Ultraviolet rays are a type of radiation from the Sun that we cannot see. The energy in these rays is harmful, causing sunburn, even cancer. Fortunately, the ozone gas in the atmosphere prevents most of these rays from reaching Earth.

WAVES THAT YOU HEAR

A vapor cloud appears around a fighter jet as it breaks the sound barrier

SOUND IS CREATED BY VIBRATION

When you knock on a door or pluck the strings of a guitar, you start vibrations. These are sound waves. Sound waves travel through the air, water, and even solid objects. Different sounds have their own unique wave size and shape. That is how our brain recognizes them.

Reflected wave

Wave

HAVE YOU EVER WONDERED . . .

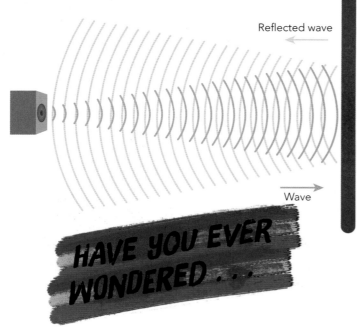

WHAT CAUSES SOUND TO ECHO?

When sound waves are reflected back to where they started, it causes an echo. Usually sound bounces back from hard surfaces, such as walls, particularly in closed areas. Soft materials absorb sound and prevent it from traveling any farther.

Plucking the strings on a guitar causes them to vibrate and create sound waves.

Some planes travel faster than the speed of sound. When they break the sound barrier, there is a loud boom, like an explosion. This is called a sonic boom and is caused by the sound waves getting crushed together. The change in air pressure around the aircraft causes the formation of a vapor cloud, which makes it appear to be flying out of a cloud.

Underwater microphones, like the one being lowered into the ocean, can pick up sounds created many miles away.

SOUND TRAVELS AT DIFFERENT SPEEDS

The speed of sound depends on how fast the vibrations can move. Sound travels faster in water than in air. Dry air would carry vibrations 1,125 feet every second; water would take them 4,862 feet every second!

Walkie-talkies pick up radio signals.

Radio and electric signals carry sound over long distances

The microphone in a phone changes sound energy into radio signals or electricity so that it can travel farther. Radio signals are received by cell phones and walkie-talkie radios. Electric signals flow through wires between landline telephones, where a small speaker changes the electricity back into sound energy.

WATT IS ELECTRICITY

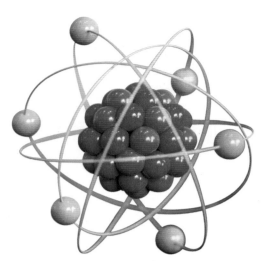

Electrons spin around the center of an atom.

THE MOVEMENT OF ELECTRONS GENERATES ELECTRICITY

Electrons are so tiny that we can't see them. They spin around the center of atoms, which are small particles that make up everything. Sometimes, when many atoms get together, electrons move from one atom to another in the same direction. This flow of electrons is called electricity.

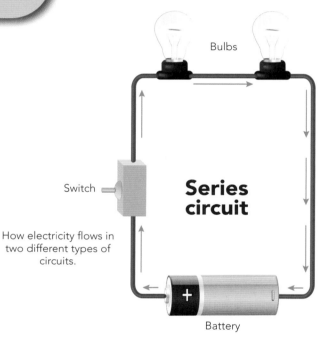

Bulbs

Switch

Series circuit

How electricity flows in two different types of circuits.

Battery

An electricity generator powered by diesel fuel

HAVE YOU EVER WONDERED . . .

HOW DO ELECTRICITY GENERATORS WORK?

They are powered by wind, water, coal, oil, diesel, gas, or nuclear fuel, and they convert this energy into electricity.

Networking

Most of our electricity is made in power stations by machines called generators. It flows into our homes, schools, and towns through cables buried beneath our feet, or wires hanging high over our heads. Electricity is measured in watts.

High power lines and towers carry electricity from power plants for distribution to homes.

Batteries for small electrical gadgets

BATTERIES CAN ALSO MAKE ELECTRICITY

Metals and other special chemicals inside a battery react together to make electricity. The chemicals are dangerous, so never open a battery to look inside it.

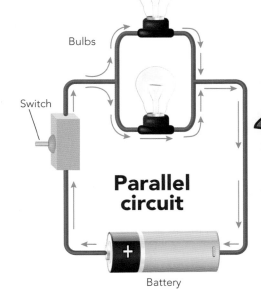

Bulbs

Switch

Parallel circuit

Battery

AMAZING!

If you stick copper wire and a steel paper clip in a lemon, the metals will mix with the lemon juice and make electricity. You could also make electricity by rubbing a balloon against a nylon sweater. This is static electricity, and it has pulling power—the balloon will stick to a wall.

Electricity can be switched off

Electricity works only when it can flow all the way around a loop called a circuit. Turning off a switch breaks the circuit, stopping the flow and turning electrical appliances off. Turning on the switch joins the circuit again.

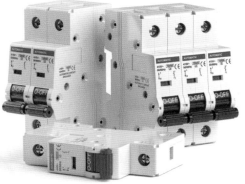

Miniature circuit breakers (MCBs) switch off automatically if there is a fault in the electrical system.

OPPOSITES ATTRACT

OPPOSITE POLES OF MAGNETS STICK TO EACH OTHER

If you have two magnets, the north pole of one will attract (pull) the south pole of the other toward it. Two north poles, or two south poles, will repel each other or will push each other away. Only a few materials have this magnetic quality, which is why most magnets are made of iron or steel. Magnets attract only other magnetic material.

Iron shavings show the pattern of a magnet's force field.

Magnets are useful at home for sticking notes to the steel door of your refrigerator.

TO DO LIST
Have a nice day!
1.
2.
3.
4.
5.
6.
7.
8.

AMAZING!

Place a bar magnet at the center of a stiff sheet of paper. Sprinkle tiny iron filings all around the magnet. Magnetic attraction will make the filings move. If you help them by tapping gently on the paper, they will form a clear pattern around the magnet—showing its force field.

Magnets create an invisible force field

Magnets work because they have an invisible force called magnetism, which pulls inward. Magnetism creates a magnetic field all around, but the force is greatest at the ends of the magnets, which are its north and south poles.

The red (north) point of the compass needle swings toward Earth's North Pole.

HAVE YOU EVER WONDERED . . .

HOW TO FIND YOUR WAY IF YOU'RE LOST

Use a compass. This is a small device that can fit in your pocket. It has a magnetic needle, which spins freely—and, if a magnet can move freely, its north pole, which is the back end of the compass needle, will always be pulled toward Earth's magnetic South Pole. So the front end of the compass needle will always point toward Earth's magnetic North Pole, helping you to figure out directions and find your way.

Paper clips stick to both poles of this simple electromagnet.

ELECTRICITY CAN CREATE A MAGNET

Running electricity through iron, by wrapping a wire around it, can create a powerful magnet. This is called electromagnetism, and electromagnets can be switched on and off. The most important use of such magnets is in electric motors, which run all sorts of devices—from doorbells and fans, to computers.

OUR
ENDANGERED
WORLD

THERE IS ONLY ONE EARTH

The Spix's macaw of Brazil is one bird species to have become extinct in the wild in recent years.

EARTH IS SPECIAL

As far as we know, Earth is the only planet that has life on it—and it's been here for approximately 3.5 billion years! Some of Earth's animals and plants could survive without breathing air, but none could live without water. Earth is the only planet in the solar system that has plenty of liquid water on its surface—oceans full of it!

Humans have endangered Earth

Human activities and lifestyles have created many problems for Earth, such as widespread pollution of land, water, and air, leading to global warming, and overuse of natural resources. Humans have upset the delicate balance on Earth.

Earth is a beautiful planet, and it must be preserved.

AMAZING!

Sadly, because of the negative impact of human activity, many animals are in danger. Millions of different animals live on Earth—it's their planet, as well as ours. An oil spill at sea harms seals, fish, and birds. When forests are cut down, many animals lose their homes. It's said that one kind of animal becomes extinct every 30 minutes because of what we're doing to the planet.

The scars of open mining on Earth's surface

THE DAMAGE GOES DEEP

Used to extract rocks or minerals, open-pit mining is a method that involves digging out huge amounts of earth and vegetation. Harmful natural radioactive elements that would otherwise remain buried are released during this process.

HAVE YOU EVER WONDERED . . .

CAN EARTH BE SAVED?

It can. Scientific studies indicate that though it will take a long time to clean up and turn back the clock, it is not too late to fix the damage we have caused.

SAVE THE WORLD

An illustration created for World Environment Day

DEVASTATION BY WATER AND FIRE

FLOODING CAN DROWN AN ENTIRE LANDSCAPE

When it rains very heavily or for a long time, rivers can no longer contain the extra water. They burst their banks and flood surrounding land. Along the coast, floods can happen in stormy weather when high tides or gigantic waves sweep onto the shore. In 1993 the Mississippi River, USA, flooded almost 80,778 square miles, an area the size of Greece.

In 2015 the Ob River in Russia flooded the town of Nizhnevartovsk.

Aerial view of a raging wildfire

WILDFIRES CAN GOBBLE UP THOUSANDS OF TREES

Because trees make for a ready source of fuel, wildfires can sweep through forests, leaving devastation in their wake. Fires in grasslands or scrublands can be just as bad. Wildfires can be started by lightning or volcanic eruptions. Unfortunately, most are caused by human carelessness—cigarette butts and campfires.

Beware the tsunami

Created by a sudden movement of water due to an earthquake, a volcanic eruption, or even a glacier breaking off, these are huge and powerful waves. They can travel long distances at speeds of over 310 miles per hour. As the waves reach the shore, the shallower waters cause them to pile up and grow taller, at times reaching the height of a seven-story building! When they crash down on land, the amount and force of the water smashes and washes everything away.

A fearsome tsunami struck the coast of Thailand in 2004.

HAVE YOU EVER WONDERED . . .

WHAT IS A FLASH FLOOD?

Flash floods happen when a large amount of water suddenly enters a small river, or sometimes even a dry riverbed. It could be because of a sudden deluge, or a dam that bursts. Flash floods can happen in the desert too, during a rare downpour.

Helicopters are used to douse forest fires by "bombing" them with water.

AMAZING!

Forest fires are very difficult to put out. They move at over six miles per hour, sparks leaping from tree to tree, and can even jump across roads and rivers. The wind may change direction and there is no saying where it may blow the fire. Even when you think a fire is dead, the embers may shoot out another spark.

GLOBAL CLIMATE CHANGE

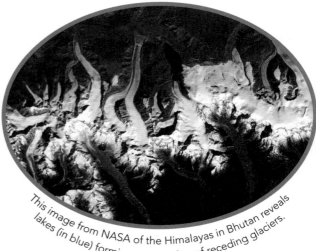

This image from NASA of the Himalayas in Bhutan reveals lakes (in blue) forming at the edge of receding glaciers.

TEMPERATURES ARE RISING

Climate change means an alteration in climatic factors like rainfall and temperature over the long term. This is happening in all regions of Earth. Scientists can clearly see that, despite some really cold winters, there has been a steady increase in Earth's average temperatures over the past 150 years.

Experts around the world are studying climate change.

GLOBAL WARMI...

HAVE YOU EVER WONDERED . . .

IS CLIMATE CHANGE CONTROLLABLE?

Most scientists think it is. However, it will need people to make a lot of changes in the way they live, produce, and consume things. Adoption of green technologies will play a big role.

AMAZING!

Polar ice is very important in the formation of the currents that move warm water from the equator to the poles, and cold water back to the equator. These currents affect climate, and therefore life on land as well as in the oceans.

Even a little is too much

Earth's surface is nearly 1.8°F warmer than it was 250 years ago. That may not feel like much to your body, but the global effect of this small increase is huge. Summers have been getting hotter, over the last few decades, everywhere in the world. Parts of the world that were permanently frozen are shrinking as the ice melts.

Melting icebergs are raising sea levels.

Deadly changes

Climate change is destroying ecosystems, the natural environments in which all living things, including us, depend on. As oceans warm up, coral reefs are dying, impacting the fish that live in them. Forest fires are more frequent due to hotter weather, incinerating many species of trees, affecting the birds, insects, and other animals that depend on them.

Coral reefs are bleaching and dying.

A flooded settlement in Texas, USA

CLIMATE-RELATED DISASTERS ARE ON THE INCREASE

Raging fires have burned large areas of forest across the globe. Hurricanes have swept across countries causing destruction. There have been floods in places that have never experienced them before, and heatwaves are becoming more common in Europe.

RISING TEMPERATURES

GASES IN EARTH'S ATMOSPHERE TRAP THE SUN'S HEAT

Earth has just the right temperature to support life. Some gases, called greenhouse gases, are especially effective in trapping heat. By burning "fossil fuels"—coal, oil, and natural gas—we are putting more greenhouse gases into the atmosphere, causing the planet to grow warmer.

Sun

Greenhouse gases

CO_2 LEVELS HAVE BEEN CLIMBING

For over 650,000 years of human history, CO_2 levels stayed at about 300 parts per million particles (ppm) of air. It is only in the last 150 years that they have shot up to 412 ppm. Scientists believe that around 350 ppm would be a much better level for the good of Earth and our own health.

AMAZING!

The Antarctic and Greenland ice sheets together hold 99 percent of Earth's frozen fresh water. If the Antarctic ice sheet alone were to melt, the sea would rise by 200 feet. Coastlines would change all over the world, and some islands, in the Maldives, for example, could disappear completely!

Devices like air purifiers have become popular to keep the air clean inside homes.

Some of the Maldive islands are in danger of being submerged if ice sheets melt and sea levels rise.

The right amount of the Sun's heat gets trapped by natural greenhouse gases, but humans release more greenhouse gases than is good for the atmosphere, in the form of aerosol particles made up of smoke and other pollutants.

Plants play a crucial role

Plants and trees, even plankton in the oceans, help to balance the greenhouse effect. They take harmful carbon dioxide from the atmosphere to make energy. But, not only are humans putting more CO_2 in the atmosphere, they are cutting down forests, too.

Greenhouse gases

Aerosols

The greenhouse effect is increasing

The way that we—the 7.7 billion people on Earth today—lead our lives increases the amount of carbon dioxide (CO_2) in the atmosphere. CO_2 is a greenhouse gas—too much CO_2 in the air warms Earth.

As the world's population has increased, so have greenhouse gases.

HAVE YOU EVER WONDERED . . .

WHAT IS A CARBON FOOTPRINT?

The amount of carbon dioxide you put into the atmosphere is your carbon footprint. There are many ways to reduce it, such as biking or walking instead of driving a car, or eating locally grown food that does not have to be transported over long distances.

Biking to work reduces your carbon footprint.

POLLUTING THE AIR WE BREATHE

SMOKE IN CITIES HAS LONG BEEN KNOWN TO BE HARMFUL

In 1306 King Edward I of England introduced what was possibly the first environmental law and tried to ban coal. He realised that burning coal produced too much smoke, which hung over the city like a poisonous cloud. Centuries later, the steam engine was invented, which powered the Industrial Revolution—and with it came even more air pollution!

Industrial chimneys pollute the air over a city.

AMAZING!

Air pollution happens when a lot of harmful particles, gases, and chemicals enter the atmosphere. These make our eyes burn, and breathing becomes difficult as well as harmful. The World Health Organization says 2.4 million people die each year because of air pollution. Cars are the single biggest category of pollutants in the world today.

The air is so bad in some cities that people have to wear masks to filter out harmful particles.

Fossil fuels are the biggest culprit

Fossil fuels form from the remains of ancient plants and animals, buried deep within the earth. Heat and pressure change their decomposed remains into coal, oil, and natural gas. These are non-renewable resources because they take millions of years to form and deposits on Earth are being used up fast. When burned, fossil fuels release gases that harm the environment.

Coal

Damage caused by acid rain to a statue in Germany

SULPHUR DIOXIDE (SO$_2$) IS ANOTHER HARMFUL GAS

SO$_2$ is also released by burning fossil fuels, but, unlike CO$_2$, it is not a greenhouse gas. It is very acidic, which means it eats away at surfaces. In the atmosphere, it mixes with droplets of moisture to make acid rain, which causes sickness, even death, in both plants and animals.

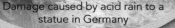

HAVE YOU EVER WONDERED . . .

CAN GASES PROTECT US?

Ozone forms a layer of helpful gas in Earth's atmosphere. It protects us from the Sun's dangerous ultraviolet rays. Unfortunately, the ozone layer has been damaged because humans have put harmful chemicals called chlorofluorocarbons (CFCs) into the atmosphere. Even though products that release these chemicals are no longer used as much, the damage has already been done.

A hole in the ozone layer over Antarctica repaired itself dramatically in 2019 but it remains to be seen whether it lasts.

POLLUTING THE WATER

WATER CARRIES EVERYTHING OUT OF SIGHT

Perhaps that is why areas of water have always been used to dump waste. But growing amounts of waste, which cannot be broken down and digested by bacteria in water, are now clogging up water systems all over the world.

Pesticides contribute to water pollution

Waste water full of chemicals from factories flows directly into rivers, but pesticides used on farms and in gardens also find their way down into ground water, poisoning it. Often, this is the same water we drink.

Mining activities release large amounts of iron, copper, and acid into the Rio Tinto in Spain, coloring it red.

AMAZING!

Plastic waste in the oceans kills millions of marine animals each year. Some are strangled by fishing nets; others choke on plastic bags. All kinds of sea creatures, from the largest of whales to tiny plankton, are eating microplastics. Approximately nine million tons of plastic ends up in the oceans every year.

Carelessly discarded plastic bags, bottles, and styrofoam containers litter our oceans.

Sewage can be a killer

Every day, all across the world, sewage is dumped into streams and rivers. Bacteria in the water act to break down and digest the sewage, but they use oxygen in the process. Fish start dying when sewage levels increase since there is no oxygen left in the water for them to breathe.

Sewage flows into a stream.

HAVE YOU EVER WONDERED . . .

IS IT POSSIBLE TO CLEAN UP THE OCEANS?

Some people have invented ways of trapping larger pieces of plastic floating in the ocean, but the major problem is that sunlight, wind, and waves break down plastic waste into tiny particles. These microplastics are impossible to recover, and are found in every corner of the globe, and inside marine and land animals.

An oil spill on Koh Samet, Thailand, being cleaned up with suction pumps and pipes.

OIL SPILLS HAVE CREATED HAVOC

There have been many instances of disastrous water pollution by oil spills over the years. Caused by a crack and an explosion on an off-shore oil rig, the Gulf of Mexico oil spill in 2010 affected some 1,300 miles of the US coast from Texas to Florida. Its victims ranged from fish to birds.

TRASHING PLANET EARTH

Rusty drums with chemical waste can leak and create toxicity.

GARBAGE IS A PROBLEM

Homes generate huge amounts of garbage; factories generate even more. Because so much trash is made, it's a problem to deal with it all. Some is burned inside furnaces—which pollutes the air. A lot is buried in the land—which pollutes the land. Only some is collected and sent for recycling.

HAVE YOU EVER WONDERED . . .

WHAT DOES "BIODEGRADABLE" MEAN?

Something that is made of organic material and will decay and decompose to become part of the environment again is said to be biodegradable. Banana peel is biodegradable, so is paper, but glass is not.

Garbage disposal workers in Agbogbloshie, Ghana

Banana peels can be easily decomposed by nature.

Trash poisons

Much of what is thrown away as trash pollutes the soil. This is particularly true for industrial waste, a lot of which is chemical. Toxic chemicals enter the soil, poisoning it, and causing plants and animals to die.

Styrofoam never decomposes.

Some waste will never disappear

The amount of time garbage takes to decompose depends on what it is made of. Generally speaking, the more processed a material, the longer it takes to decompose. Paper takes about a month to decompose; a plastic bag about 20 years. Materials such as styrofoam are not degradable. They will be around forever!

LANDFILLS GET BIGGER EVERY DAY

Huge dumps where piles of trash are collected are called landfills. Many of these are serious environmental health hazards, although ways are being found to make the landfills more efficient and prevent the trash from polluting either the land or air.

Landfills become bigger and bigger until they have to be treated.

AMAZING!

Many developed countries ship their waste, particularly plastic waste, to poorer countries to dispose of.

Agbogbloshie in Ghana has become the biggest dump for e-waste. Computers, TVs, refrigerators, and electronics from all over the world end up here. People processing the waste are frequently sick with headaches and nausea. Some have died young of cancers caused by the harmful substances in the waste.

CLEAN, RENEWABLE ENERGY

THE NATURAL WORLD HAS EVERYTHING WE NEED

Burning fossil fuels to make machines work causes pollution. But nature has many energy sources that do not pollute, or pollute very little, such as windmills. Also, unlike fossil fuels, which are limited resources, these sources cannot be used up: they renew themselves.

Windmill farms like this are used to harness wind energy.

The heat energy captured from natural geysers in Iceland is used to heat homes.

HAVE YOU EVER WONDERED . . .

IS IT POSSIBLE TO TAP EARTH'S HEAT?

In Iceland, which has more than 25 volcanoes and numerous hot springs, many buildings and swimming pools are heated with geothermal hot water. Today, the USA is the world's largest producer of geothermal electricity.

Harness the wind

Windmills are not a new idea. They used to dot the countryside of many countries. Today, the idea is being used in the form of wind turbines. Standing over 300 feet tall, they generate electricity from the wind.

MOVING WATER CREATES POWER

Dams across rivers use the power of flowing water to spin turbines and generate electricity. This is called hydroelectricity—the word "hydro" means water in Greek. Along the coast, the power of crashing waves and the tides is also being harnessed for energy that is clean and renewable.

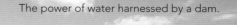

The power of water harnessed by a dam.

A biogas plant in the Czech Republic

AMAZING!

Plants create their own energy, and this energy can be used to make fuel such as ethanol and biodiesel. Also, when plant and other organic matter rots, it emits a gas called methane, which can be used to make compressed natural gas (CNG), a cleaner fuel than petroleum and coal. What this means is that trash rotting in landfills can be used as an energy source!

The power of the Sun

The Sun produces more energy in a single hour than all the people on Earth use in a year. Solar panels capture the Sun's energy and turn it into electricity without polluting Earth's air and water. Solar power is already being used to light streets, heat homes, and even power cars.

Solar panels can be installed on the roof of your home.

REDUCE, REUSE, RECYCLE

Reduce means to use less of something.
Reuse means to use something again.
To recycle is to save something so it can be made into a new thing. It is really quite a simple way to contribute toward our Earth's well-being.

The universal symbol for "recycling"

HAVE YOU EVER WONDERED . . .

WHAT MORE CAN I DO FOR PLANET EARTH?

If you would like to help make the Earth a better, safer place to live, now and in the future, you might like to join an environmental group such as Greenpeace, Friends of the Earth, or World Wide Fund for Nature. You can find their addresses at your local library or on the Internet. You can make a difference.

Recycling can reduce the amount of waste generated.

Save the Plane

PLASTIC   METAL

All sorts of materials can be recycled

To make it easier, it is better to separate different materials—plastic in one container; glass in another; paper, newspapers, and magazines in another; and so on. If you put in cans or milk cartons with newspaper, for example, it would make the recycling messy.

Compost bin for a family garden

A metal mug and thermos

GLASS

PAPER

AMAZING!

Vegetable peelings, tea leaves, and grass clippings are "green" waste. If you pile them into a pile in the garden, they will rot down to make compost. Compost is food for the soil. It contains nutrients that keep the soil healthy.

GET A METAL OR GLASS THERMOS

Plastic products such as water bottles and plastic shopping bags make up a lot of plastic waste. Make sure you don't add to it. These are all small but major steps, and lots of people are already taking them.

Small changes can make a big difference.

Turn off electrical items after use

That's a good way to start using less. Another is not to waste anything, particularly water: don't leave taps dripping. Biking is energy-efficient and good exercise—much better than taking the car.